Truth, Dare, Double Dare, Promise or Repeat

ALSO BY MONICA LEE

The Percussionist's Wife: A Memoir of Sex, Crime & Betrayal

*How to Look Hot & Feel Amazing in your 40s:
The 21-Day Age-Defying Diet, Exercise
& Everything Makeover Plan*

Truth, Dare, Double Dare, Promise or Repeat

On Finding the Meaning of "Like" in 1982

MONICA LEE

BOOKS

TRUTH, DARE, DOUBLE DARE, PROMISE OR REPEAT
Copyright © 2017 Monica Lee
All rights reserved. No part of this book may be used or reproduced in any manner whatsoever without written permission except in the case of brief quotations embodied in critical articles and reviews.

ISBN 978-0-9861943-2-0

Design by Monica Lee
Cover image © kryzhov, used under license from Shutterstock.com

MINDFULMONICA.WORDPRESS.COM

To Jill
For being a voice of reason
(with a sense of humor)
not only in high school
but all through life

CONTENTS

Introduction	1
Cast of Characters	7
Chapter 1	11
Chapter 2	19
Chapter 3	27
Chapter 4	35
Chapter 5	41
Chapter 6	49
Chapter 7	57
Chapter 8	65
Chapter 9	71
Chapter 10	79
Chapter 11	87
Chapter 12	99

Chapter 13	111
Chapter 14	119
Chapter 15	137
Chapter 16	151
Chapter 17	171
Chapter 18	183
Chapter 19	193
Chapter 20	205
Chapter 21	217
Chapter 22	223
Chapter 23	231
Chapter 24	241
Epilogue	253
Acknowledgments	261
About the Author	263
Reading Guide for Moms & Daughters	265

INTRODUCTION

I DON'T REMEMBER the details of my first kiss. I don't remember if his lips were soft or if his breath smelled sweet. I don't remember if my palms were sweaty or if I closed my eyes. In fact, I only remember my first kiss at all because I have it recorded in my eighth-grade diary, a small pink polka-dotted book with a sweet illustration on the front of a girl seated at her desk and the words, "Thank you, Lord, for every new day." It had a lock but it could be picked with a paper clip. Inside I wrote, "We played Truth, Dare, Double Dare, Promise or Repeat. Craig got dared and he had to kiss me. Oh for gross!!! It was the pits! Gross! Dirty! This is the first time I ever kissed a boy, and I am sad it happened on a dare."

I wrote in that diary every day. Most of the time I was recording who was gossiping about whom, what clothes I wanted to buy, how stupid my parents were and other banal events that seemed eminently important to a teenage girl growing up in a small town tucked among fields of corn and soybeans in central Minnesota.

After writing my first memoir about my first marriage and how it went so catastrophically off the rails, I got nostalgic for the simplicity of my first loves—or, more appropriately labeled, "likes"—and started reading the diaries I had kept so devotedly when the "boy crazies" infected my teenage mind. I was surprised at how surprised I was as I read. After all, I had written the entries in the first place. I had experienced all those intense feelings. How could I have forgotten them? What I remembered as simple was, oh-so-complex. I was surprised, too, by all the obvious signals boys were sending me that eluded me at the time and all the mistakes I, regrettably, was doomed to repeat. How naïve I had been. But hidden among all my blind blunders regarding my burgeoning sexuality and opposite-sex liaisons, I was surprised to find the seeds of many truths I still held dear, even after decades of experience in kissing, relationships and marriage.

The stories deserved to be told, complete with all their teenage drama and romance, and *Truth, Dare, Double Dare, Promise or Repeat* was born. I wrote this book for every teenager trying to navigate the maze of finding true love, or at least true "like," and for every woman who grew up in the '80s who might have forgotten all she learned during those seemingly simpler times.[1]

Except for the names, all the diary entries in this book are actual excerpts from the journals I kept in high school. Wadena, Minnesota, is a real place, and I went to school there in 1982. The events described in the narrative of this book actually occurred though I rearranged and compressed the occurrence of some of them to create a better story. Most of the people exist, too, but some of them

---

[1] In fact, this book might be just the thing for sparking conversations about birds, bees and boys in a moms-and-daughters book club.

will invariably take issue with how I remember them; I changed most of their names and created composites for some of the more nefarious characters. The dialogue in this book is mostly fictionalized; entire conversations were created using only a line or two from my diary. The story I tell here is designed to recreate my emotions as I remember them. As Buddhist author Nichiren Daishonin has said, "It is the heart that is important."[2]

Back to that first kiss. "Craig" was Craig Davidson. His most distinctive feature was his red hair, but in my junior-high classification system, which valued height over any other characteristic, he was "one of the taller boys in my grade"—not as tall as I was, but close.

It was impressive, at least to me, to be as tall as I was in eighth grade in 1981. I was already 5-foot-8, having inherited my father's tall and lanky frame, and I towered over almost everyone no matter their gender. At that age, my height put me at an advantage for only one thing: it qualified me to play basketball, an activity my parents insisted on imposing on me even though I had no ball-handling skills and a vertical jump that barely cleared a tuna can.

In the way the word "like" carried weighty connotations, Craig "liked" me, though I wasn't entirely aware of it at the time. Earlier in the year, when I gave a bag of Hershey's Kisses for Valentine's Day to Brent Gorgonzola, my obsession du jour, Craig gave me a box, wrapped like a special gift. Inside was a bold note that said, "I want to go steady with you." I was surprised because, most of the time, Craig had been trying to get me to flirt more with Brent. What did "go steady" mean, anyway? I wrote back a note that said I was flattered, but no. I was worried I would hurt his feelings, but then

---

[2] If you like this memoir, then the liberties I've taken with the truth will be worth it. If you don't, you can tell everyone the Introduction was the best part of the book.

we talked about it, and he wasn't mad at me at all. Or, at least, he *said* he wasn't. He was probably dying inside. But from my self-centered perspective, everything was hunky-dory after that. Sometimes I would go to his house to play basketball in his driveway with him and the neighbors, and sometimes I watched him play Dungeons & Dragons with other nerdy boys who were our mutual friends.

Looking back, it was perhaps Craig who conspired with someone to be dared to kiss me at all. I was oblivious to any backroom machinations there may have been.

Was it literally "gross"? I doubt Craig would have pressed his tongue into my mouth at that stage (I certainly would have informed Dear Diary of that development!), so my first kiss with a boy was unlikely anything more than a chaste union of his lips and mine for a second or two. What was "gross" was the situation and the audience. Rather than a private kiss shared to seal some pact of "like" or love, it was a public display of affection performed entirely to satisfy the hunger of a blood-thirsty audience of thirteen- and fourteen-year-olds. The thought of being stared at—by the crowd, or even by Craig—made me want to crawl out of my skin. And maybe my use of the word "gross" was my intuition talking: Craig turned out to be an odd bird with more than a healthy obsession with me.

Unfortunately, one can't romanticize one's first kiss when it's recorded in ball-point pen in the pages of a diary.

Fortunately, I caught on to the whole kissing thing soon enough. The kiss performed on a dare was the prelude to learning how to kiss—actually kiss—the year I turned fifteen. Navigating relationships and learning the meaning of like—or love—was far trickier. It's a skill I would venture to say I haven't mastered even in my forties. But looking back on that fateful year devoted almost exclusively to reeling in a keeper boyfriend like so much walleye illuminates my inner life and my self-esteem even now.

CAST OF CHARACTERS

Jill: Best friend (the sensible yet funny one)

Amy: Best friend (and chief rival)

Cindy: Best friend (the one who was always willing to tagalong)

Valerie Stonyridge: Naughty Girl in my circle of friends

Tonya Palamino: Nasty Girl definitely not in my circle of friends

Mick Bierbrauer: Best friend of the opposite sex

Brent Gorgonzola (a.k.a. Brent-the-Cheese): On-again, off-again love interest of the jock variety

Scott Briller: On-again, off-again love interest of the brainy variety

Craig Davidson: I never returned his romantic interest in me

Todd Byrd (a.k.a. Todd-the-God): He never returned my romantic interest in him

Reeve Koroso: Homecoming King material on the lines of Todd-the-God, only older

Royce Koroso: Reeve's little brother

Brian Flourman: Family friend of surprising talents

October 5, 1981

Dear Diary,

I love music. Every song I hear reminds me of a guy or a dance or a time or something. I just thought I'd write that …

Scott (of all people) said I have nice fingernails. Freak my mind away! (That's Amy's saying.) We were in science doing some stupid mountains. Wow! Now I have a whole list of guys I like: Todd Washington, Wayne, (I kinda have my eye on David Green), Brent, Scott, David Levine, Todd Byrd. Wow, what a list. Hmm.

1

"HOW ON EARTH did one blue shoe get into my locker?" I thought as I dug through a blizzard of teenage artifacts looking for my notes for science class. I was puzzled, and I didn't like mysteries. Pulling a shoe out of my locker that should have been under a pile in my bedroom was bewildering. I hadn't worn those shoes since the last week before school got out for Christmas.

They were my favorite shoes. Made in China, they were purchased at a mall in Winnipeg—another country!—where everything was different and special. Bright blue satin-covered ballet flats with round toes and skinny ankle straps, the shoes did not add to my height and that was their greatest virtue because I generally looked over the scruffy heads of all the boys in my grade except Scott Briller, who had told me earlier in the week that I had nice fingernails when we were working together in science class on a worksheet about mountains. They were cute, the shoes (some of the boys were, too, but I wished all of them were taller).

All the ninth graders' lockers were on the third floor of Wadena Junior High School, an ancient brick structure built in the early twentieth century. The whole building rumbled during the five minutes between classes, when hundreds of pubescent teenagers moved from room to room. Seventh graders' lockers were in the basement, eighth graders' on the second floor, and ninth graders' on top. The school year was half over and soon I'd be on the bottom of the pecking order again when I became a tenth grader at the senior high school, so I had only four more months to enjoy my ninth-grade status.

My locker was a pigsty, like pretty much everything else in my domain, including my bedroom.[3] No wonder Jill wouldn't share a locker with me. Only my Bonnie Belle lip gloss—purchased and worn for decorative purposes only—was on the top shelf. Everything else—my school books, my notebooks, my dirty gym clothes, my coat, stocking hat and mittens—was in a mammoth pile in the bottom of the locker. I received new gloves for Christmas, so my mittens shouldn't have been in there at all, and my gym clothes should have been taken home and washed over Christmas break, but back then I hated cleaning even more than I do now.

Wow, that's where my personal narrative for Mr. O's English class had been hiding! I thought as I pulled it from the detritus. *Good thing I found that.* It was due Friday. Mr. O gave us a fill-in-the-blank assignment so it was easy to complete, but I hadn't turned it in yet.

---

[3] A disdain for cleaning followed me into adulthood, giving rise to more than one resentful roommate (including the ones to whom I was married). When Jill and I lived together in college and fought repeatedly about dirty dishes and trash removal, she finally resorted to providing me with a detailed checklist for cleaning the bathroom once a week. If I can clean a bathroom at all as an adult, I have Jill to thank.

My name is Monica Lee Wallgren. My little brother used to call me 'Ca and my little sister calls me Moni, but you're not related to me. Please call me Monica.

I like Brent Gorgonzola, food, my cat, clothes, tennis shoes and Judy Blume books. Oh, and rock-and-roll music.

I hate George Gordon, hyper dogs like my friend Amy's wiener dog, sometimes (almost always) my parents, low-heeled dress shoes[4] and books with small print.

This year in school I am taking drafting class with twelve boys, and I love it. I've only "gone with" one guy since fall and he was a seventh grader and I didn't honestly like him so he doesn't count. I went to several school dances, and I wish I would dance more at them. I hate almost all my teachers (sorry, Mr. O, not you), and I'm getting straight-A grades in every class except gym.

Where is my other blue shoe?

At that time in my life I knew what I liked, and I knew what I didn't like or at least I was arrogant enough to *think* I knew. I liked boys. I didn't like mysteries. I only wished the boys I liked liked me. But sometimes I couldn't blame them. I could be rude and bossy and loud. Sometimes, my friends didn't like me, and sometimes I didn't even like myself.

---

[4] The editor in me nudges me to substitute "cleaning" for "low-heeled dress shoes" in the list of things I hated. I loved those blue flats and there was no reason they should have been lost in my locker.

I wondered if I should change the line about hating my teachers but I didn't have time to worry about it. I didn't have time to worry about my other blue shoe either as I handled its mysterious lonely mate. I had to get to Mr. Jefferson's science class by 10:35. I threw the shoe back into my mess, slammed the locker shut and whizzed the knob on the lock. I lifted the handle to make sure it was secure, and I hurried off to join the throng going down the steps to Mr. Jefferson's classroom.

+ + +

Mr. Jefferson was standing in the doorway to his class, as he did between all classes, every day. He looked a bit like Superman, only shorter and with more padding. "Nice shirt, Wallgren," he said, using my last name as he did for all his students. "You look like you should enlist."

I was wearing a drab green Army button-up, purchased during Christmas vacation for the sole purpose of impressing Scott Briller. He was into punk rock, which I didn't understand at all. How can you like the music when you don't understand the words? Somewhere in my mind, my Army shirt connected to the punk trend. "Thanks," I said as I squeezed through the doorway, not quite catching Mr. Jefferson's humor. I liked Mr. Jefferson's class, but I couldn't always tell if Mr. Jefferson liked me.

I smiled at Scott Briller and slid into my seat at the table directly in front of him. He didn't say a word about my attire.

While we were diagramming the differences between igneous rock, sedimentary rock and metamorphic rock, I felt someone touch my neck. I spun around in my seat, and saw Scott holding a scissors in one hand and a lock of my hair in the other.

"What did you do?!" I yelled, standing up and wildly groping the back of my hair. "Did you cut my *hair?!*"

The smirk on Scott's face melted away when he realized how angry I was.

"OK, that's enough, love birds," Mr. Jefferson said. "Hand me the scissors, Briller, and you can move your butt right here." Mr. Jefferson pointed at the empty chair in the front row, within spitting distance of Mr. Jefferson's lecture.

"I'm sorry," Scott said softly, gathering up his books and notebooks.

"I can't believe you cut my hair," I said, shaking my head.

Scott looked as if he was going to cry. Or maybe it was my imagination. I kicked myself later for throwing such a snit about a strand of hair.

+ + +

Mondays, Wednesdays and Fridays were my favorite days of the week because I had band. The other percussionists and I stood right behind the cornet players, including Todd Byrd, whom I liked to refer to as Todd-the-God. But I liked Tuesdays and Thursdays, too, because I had choir with Todd, and he sat only one table away during lunch period right after.

Despite missing the opportunity to ogle Todd-the-God during John Philip Sousa marches, I skipped band practice that Wednesday to work on the yearbook. I was a co-editor of the yearbook with Krista, a sweet and competent partner who knew enough not to argue with me when I offered up a brilliant idea. Later, some of the drummers in band asked me where I was and teased me about skipping out. I was flattered they noticed I was gone. And I wondered if Todd-the God noticed, but I doubted it.

In drafting class, I wrote a poem before I tried flirting with Brent:

> There once was a teacher named Fred.
> The students, his class they did dread.
> The word that he used
> That kept them amused
> Not graphed, but grafted, instead.

"Whatcha workin' on?" I whispered to Brent after Mr. Rockman with his military crew cut and equally militaristic disciplinary style walked by.

"Drafting." He rolled his eyes. "Duh."

"I know, but Project A or Project B?"

"That's for me to know and you to find out," he said.

OK, this was going nowhere.

I tried again as I doodled in the margins of my graph paper. "I'm working on A."

The bell rang, signally the end of class.

"Well, good for you, goodie two-shoes," he said, scooping up his paper and pencils. "I was working on B because B is for Brent and B is for best, and I'm the best."

This time *I* rolled my eyes. *What a conceited jerk.* "Yup, you're the best," I said, and I walked out of Mr. Rockman's classroom. Brent was one of those mysteries I professed to dislike. I could never read his signals. At the Homecoming dance earlier in the year, while strains of Lionel Richie telling Diana Ross he wanted to share all his endless love with her played in the background, I had told him straight out "I like you." And then my face flushed and I stared at my feet. "Don't be embarrassed," he said so sweetly then.[5] Where was *that* Brent?

A few minutes after the drafting class poured out into the hallway, I saw Brent leaning against the wall and putting his head down like he regretted something he had said.

---

[5] Though I had no proof of it yet, I sensed that sex was not supposed to be an embarrassing truth-or-dare kiss shared in public and that the evidence of love was not found in risky hair-cutting tricks or rude comebacks.

January 4, 1981

Dear Diary,

Tomorrow school starts again after two full weeks. Maybe I am getting second thoughts about going back.

Amy came back from Florida today. I haven't written about her yet because she has been gone. You will hear a lot more about her. Today, her favorite saying was "I got totally burnt." But she was extremely brown.

2

I WAS THE TALLEST girl in ninth grade if you didn't count Amy, and I didn't count Amy because she was my best friend. Or one of them anyway. Amy was 5-foot-8, too, but she was blonde and attractive so it seemed like she fulfilled her height in ways I never did.

At that moment when cold winds were whipping across the barren plains, she was tan, too, and being tan when every other person in Minnesota was pale white was a status symbol. She had just returned from Christmas vacation in Florida, and I was not impressed.

"Guess who's back in town?" Jill said when she called me.

"Who?" I played along.

"Amy is home from Florida!"

"Oh, goodie," I said glumly, eyeing my pale forearms while I cupped the phone in the crook of my neck. I never looked forward to the inevitable comparison of our skin tones.

"She said she's totally burnt," Jill said.

"You'd think she'd learn," I responded. Amy's dad was the superintendent of the technical school, and her family escaped

Minnesota's bitterly cold weather for a few weeks every year during Christmas vacation.[6]

Jill was my best friend, too. She was tall and lean (but not as tall as I was) and she was naturally blonde, like Amy, but she wasn't tan so I didn't think she was as cute. Jill's gift was humor. She was always making me laugh.

Instead of basking in the sun, Jill and I had spent most of Christmas vacation either playing basketball or keeping score for the boys basketball team. Playing basketball was required by my parents, who insisted I participate in at least one sport every school year even though whatever grace and coordination I possessed was limited to the intellectual realm. Keeping score for the boys team was my idea so that I could keep an eye on Todd Byrd and Brent Gorgonzola.

Todd rhymed with "God," and that was no coincidence because Todd was the cutest boy in the entire junior high. Wow. He was in eighth grade but he played with the ninth graders because he handled a basketball like it was an extension of his hand, and his shooting accuracy was unparalleled. He was tall, and you could see his arm muscles—he had biceps *and* triceps. He had one of those strong chins like Sylvester Stallone that jutted out just right, but the best part was his brown hair which he wore feathered back. Sometimes his hair was greasy, and he was never even remotely cordial to me, but I thought he was divine. The first day I ever laid eyes on Todd the summer he moved to Wadena was recorded in my diary: August 25, 1981. I had been obsessed with him ever since.

---

[6] Decades later, I would come to appreciate winter escapes to warm climes, but at that point in my life I couldn't even imagine lying on a beach in December let alone feel magnanimous about Amy doing so.

When I slept over at Jill's on the night of New Year's Day, we saw Todd at the Pizza Dena.[7] The local pizza joint downtown was the hot spot in Wadena. It had gigantic retail-store-type windows facing a side street between Main Street and the Super Valu grocery store, so there was a fair amount of street traffic for a town with 5,000 residents. It was the ultimate place to see and be seen. A glass of pop served in a red textured plastic tumbler was only 45 cents, and a large pepperoni pizza was $5.99. Piping hot and crispy, pizzas were created by unseen dough makers and sauce spreaders, coming from the obscured kitchen. My friends and I spent a great deal of time crowding the booths and feeding quarters into the juke box there.

Earlier in the evening, I told Jill I hoped we'd see Todd so when we did, I couldn't believe my prescience. In retrospect, the Pizza Dena was the *only* place anyone who was anyone might be, so I shouldn't have been surprised. When I spotted him, I felt inexplicably conspicuous—I had *hoped* to see him. I don't know why I was embarrassed. No one would call me shy, but my tongue refused to move when Todd-the-God pushed open the door and sauntered by our booth.

The whole evening had a feeling of disobedience about it. Mom and Dad had no idea that Jill and I even went to the Pizza Dena that night. I was becoming more withdrawn and secretive around my parents who at this point in my life seemed like a monolithic unit, indistinct from each other like a single individual with the name MomandDad. I'd say and do anything to avoid a fight. They seemed to have an opinion on my every move—how long I stood under the shower, who I called on the phone, how I spent the money I earned

---

[7] Always described with the article "the" in front.

babysitting, how often I slept over at my friends' houses, how I performed in school and more. I argued with Dad, in particular, about everything. "I'm putting my foot down," he had said last November when he found out I went shopping to avoid accompanying the family to an RV show. While he was eying new camping digs, I fed my fashion obsession by buying a pair of jeans and colorful shoelaces with my hard-earned babysitting money. "That's it!" my Spartan father yelled when he discovered my purchases. "No more new clothes until after Christmas! I've had it! I don't even want you *talking* about clothes!" The worst rule of all? No dating until I was sixteen. Sixteen! That was a whole year away. A lifetime. I hated my parents and at the time, I thought I would hate them forever. Yet I also knew, but admitted to no one, they loved me and were looking out for me.

And then there was Brent Gorgonzola. Unlike Todd-the-God, Brent was in my grade and we had some classes together, like the aforementioned drafting class. His last name wasn't actually Gorgonzola, but it was long and complicated like the cheese; the tailor had to curve it so it would fit on the back of his basketball jersey. I memorized how to spell it by remembering it three letters at a time and all Os for vowels until the A at the end: GOR-GON-ZOL-A. Brent-the-Cheese was cute, too, and almost as tall as I was. He had a distinctive chin, sort of like Todd's, and big pouty lips. Once, we made a bet that I would kiss him twice if he made ten points in the next basketball game, and he made fourteen. But I hadn't paid up.

Brent carried a comb with a jumbo handle in his back pocket, and he was always combing his hair like he thought he was a superstar or something. It was like Shaun Cassidy's[8] hair, all feathery and

---

[8] Shaun Cassidy was a teen heartthrob I once worshipped by buying his albums and watching him solve mysteries on "The Hardy Boys."

soft looking, like it was made to run one's fingers through. I didn't think Brent was interested in me at all, even after my embarrassing confession during "Endless Love" at the Homecoming dance. At least, that's what I thought until somebody *asked* him if he liked me. He said, "Yes." That's what somebody told me. I wondered if it was true. I liked him. Didn't I?

"Don't wear black," Jill advised, bringing me back to our phone conversation. "That just makes you look whiter. What are you going wear tomorrow?"

"I don't know," I lied, winding the curly telephone cord around my fingers. I had been saving my new cream-colored pullover that I got for Christmas. The yoke had all kinds of colors, and it would coordinate with my cream-colored turtleneck, which would make me look less washed out. "I think I'll wear my Gitano jeans though."

"Have you ever seen inside of Sue Wegman's locker?" Jill asked "She keeps track of what pants Sheila Josephson wears every day."

"I would die if I didn't have enough pants to wear a different pair every day of the week," I said. I was fixated with my wardrobe of pants. Not only did I keep track of what I wore every day so I never wore the same pair twice in the same week, I was terrified of wearing what were known as high-waters and spent hours in department stores looking for pants long enough for my freakishly long inseam. Everyone made fun of Mr. Bandicot for wearing ankle-length pants. I would pretend I was sick before going to school wearing something like that.

"Get off that phone!" Dad yelled from the living room. "You've been on that thing long enough! You spend all day at school with your friends. What on God's green earth do you have to talk about for hours?"

"I've gotta go," I said.

"I know," Jill said. "Totally die if I had to wear my Chic jeans twice in one week. OK, I promised Cindy I'd call her before 8 so I've got to go, too."

"OK, bye," I said, placing the handset back in its cradle in the phone nook in the hallway.

Cindy rounded out our quartet. The four of us—me, Jill, Amy and Cindy—were best friends, but Cindy was, like a red-breasted robin in a group of colorful butterflies on Sesame Street, "one of these things that just doesn't belong." Cindy lived on the other side of town, she got more B marks than A grades, and she ran hurdles in track instead of playing basketball. And like a delicate bird, she was a sensitive soul nowhere near as brash as I was nor as courageous as Jill.

The four of us ate lunch together every day—if you'd call it lunch. Cindy was the only one who consumed the hot lunch on any sort of regular basis. She was super skinny so she ate whatever she wanted to in addition to her fingernails—she bit her nails to the quick like they were a delicacy,[9] whereas Amy and I normally only ate granola bars and drank diet Cokes while Jill made fun of us. Rumor had it that our table was called the Hamster Cage.

I stared at the phone, willing it to ring. Even though I didn't want to hear about Florida and her great tan, I wanted Amy to call me, too.

---

[9] The image of her knobby fingers with barely visible fingernails remains burned into my brain as Cindy's most distinctive feature.

January 30, 1982

Remembering January ...

School: *I still like it but I have no one to impress 'cause no one likes me! Ugh!*

Friends: *If I were my friend I'd ditch me in a minute.*

Me: *I must be gross or something! No one likes me (male or female). I want to die!*

A show: *I didn't go to any movies. Maybe that's my problem!*

3

I WAS STILL TWENTY yards from her front door when Amy leaned out and said, "Come in the house, quick! I have something for you!"

I lived five blocks away from the junior high, and she lived two blocks closer, so we walked to school together almost every day (when she wasn't skipping school to soak up the sun in Florida, that is).

I shuffled ever so slightly faster up the snow-shoveled sidewalk and ducked into her house, greeted enthusiastically by her wiener dog, Sparky.

"Yes, hello Sparky, I missed you, too."

Amy threw her arms around me in a dramatic move. "I missed you!"

"I missed you, too," I said. "Our basketball team didn't win once. We're rotten. And you didn't miss anything the first week back at school."

"I'm not worried. I got my homework assignments before Christmas vacation," she said. "I got totally burnt."

"I heard," I said.

She pushed up the sleeve of her white (of course) button-up shirt. The collar was turned up, and the waist was belted with a skinny wrap-around belt.

"Look," she said as she pressed her tan, smooth forearm against mine.

"Wow, you're so tan!" I said with my eyes opening wide, knowing that's what she wanted to hear.

"I brought you something from Florida," she said, handing me a sand dollar. "They have these all over the beach. We picked up dozens of them."

I turned the palm-sized white shell over in my hands. It was smooth and it had five small holes in it. The shell was a foreign artifact that seemed entirely out of place with the snow and the cold wind blowing through the pine trees outside and the smell of coffee and hot oatmeal inside Amy's house.

"There's a legend that goes with it," she said. "The five holes represent the five wounds of Jesus: four nail holes—one on each hand and foot—and the hole made by the spear in His side. Here's the Easter lily with the star of Bethlehem on this side," she said turning it over, "and in the middle on this side is a poinsettia. And if you break the sand dollar open, there are five white pieces of shell that look like doves."

"It's beautiful. Thanks," I said, tucking it into my backpack. "We have to get going."

On the way to school, Amy talked nonstop about her trip, which was fine by me. Even though I was jealous of her tan and her jet-set lifestyle, half-listening to her jabber made the walk to school go faster.

+ + +

"OK, girls, that does it. Run a couple of killers, and you can hit the showers," Mr. O directed when basketball practice finally ended. The "O" stood for a prototypical Norwegian last name, but no one used the whole name. Beaming with a visage a bit like Big Boy of restaurant fame, complete with the swoosh of hair, Mr. O was as friendly as his name sounded, but he was an even tougher basketball coach than he was an English teacher. "Killers" involved running up and down the basketball court, bending to touch the nearest free-throw line, half-court line, the farthest free-throw line and the far boundary at each successive turn. I hated running killers. But back then, I hated running or anything else that made me sweaty.

As we walked back to the locker room, basketballs tucked under our arms and perspiration dripping down our faces, I overheard Tonya Palomino stage whispering with a fellow guard, Valerie Stonyridge.

I remembered the time Tonya bragged to everyone that she was planning to go to California on an airplane by herself. Jealous of her bravado and perceived opportunity (if I was stuck in Wadena, everyone else should be, too!), I suggested the rest of us do a bike trip together and not invite Tonya. Tonya got mad at me and didn't talk to me for two weeks. We eventually cleared the air, but she didn't sit by us at lunch any longer. I didn't hear her secrets directly anymore; I was forced into eavesdropping to get them.

"He loved it," she said. "And we're going out again tomorrow night."

Valerie nodded.

"Boys love that stuff," said Tonya, releasing her long blonde hair from its ponytail. "They think with their dicks."

My eyes popped out of their sockets as I threw my basketball in its holding pen and made my way to my locker. *Who talks about boys' dicks like that?* I threw a shocked look at Amy, whose locker was next to mine.

Tonya and Valerie proceeded to undress and head to the showers. I never showered in the girls' locker room if I didn't have to. I, with my flat chest, felt way too exposed but Tonya with her perky round, grapefruit-sized breasts flaunted them shamelessly.

"What was that about?" I asked Amy.

"Who knows," she said, brushing her blond, wavy hair violently. "I'm mad at you."

"Why?" I said, already knowing what her beef was.

"Why didn't you throw me the ball during the round-robin drill?"

"You were never open," I lied.

"Baloney. I was open practically the whole time."

I bit my lip and concentrated on folding my sweaty T-shirt and shorts.

"I don't get you sometimes," she said, slamming her locker. "I'm leaving."

"Don't wait for me then," I said.

She didn't. We exchanged a few more heated words, and she left without me.

When I got out of the locker room a few minutes later, Jill was in the hallway putting on her down jacket.

"Walking home?" she asked.

"Sure," I said glumly, wrapping my scarf around my neck.

Walking home with Jill required a slight detour from my regular route, but I was ready for a change of scenery.

"Who was Tonya talking about at practice?" I asked Jill. She always seemed to be more plugged into the social gossip than I was.

"Reeve Koroso," she said. "I guess they're going out."

Reeve Koroso: Mr. Perfect. Two years older than we were, he was what Todd-the-God would be in a couple of years—almost tall, with beautiful hair, and a talented athlete. And he was rich by Wadena standards. His dad was a dentist.

"Tonya's going out with Reeve?" I said incredulously.

"Well, if blow jobs count as a date," Jill said.

"What do you mean, 'blow jobs'?"

"Oh my gosh, Monica, you're so dumb," Jill said. "Fellacio? Do you know what *that* is?"

"Oh," I said, drawing out the "oh" like a long tail. We walked along in silence for a few paces. Having gained all knowledge about sex from encyclopedia-like manuals stocked on library shelves that forensically defined terms but failed to define slang, I knew the definition of *fellacio*. Understanding the formal meaning did nothing for my interpretation of the act in practice. Giving head was as foreign a concept as an orgasm or homosexuality.

"Do you think you blow on it?" I asked.[10]

"I have no idea," Jill said. "And I don't want to know."

"Why was she admitting to that?" I wondered.

"She was bragging," Jill said. "Even if she's doing it, which I doubt, she shouldn't be talking about it."

"What a slut," we agreed together.

"I heard you fighting with Amy after basketball practice," Jill said, deftly changing the subject.

"I said I hated her."

---

[10] I had no older siblings, remember? And the closest I'd gotten to a girlie magazine that might explain such skills was finding one in a wind fence in a farmer's field when I was about ten (it was literally dirty, having blown against the fence for probably months). I certainly hadn't read the articles at the time.

"Nice," Jill said.

"She asked me what the Bible said about hatred."

"Good comeback," Jill said.

"Well, hate is as bad as murder," I said. I had gotten confirmed a year ago—a year before anyone else in my grade except Mick Bierbrauer. He and I were the only eighth graders in the ninth-grade confirmation class at St. John's Lutheran Church. I knew enough about the Ten Commandments to know that adultery was a sin (and fellacio was almost certainly involved in adultery) and that saying you hated someone was as damnable as actually killing them. Hate was a violation of the Fifth Commandment.

"Yup, as bad as murder," Jill said. I could feel her recrimination though she also sounded like she enjoyed it when Amy and I fought. "Why did you say you hated her?"

Amy and I were too much alike. We were both tall and skinny. We were both book smart. We cared how we looked—our clothes, our hair. And of course we both cared about boys. I was competitive. Maybe I was selfish, too. I know I was bitter.

I was jealous of Amy.[11]

She had everything: Intelligence, money, clothes, better basketball-handling skills. It *looked* like she had everything anyway. And it seemed like boys paid an inordinate amount of attention to Amy and her honey-colored hair and tan skin; I hated watching her show off her tan legs during basketball practice, which is why I wasn't throwing her the ball—I wasn't even looking at her. I knew, too, that

---

[11] To be honest, I was only vaguely aware of being jealous of Amy at the time. But when I read my diaries with the clear-headed perspective of experience three decades later, it was obvious I longed to be like Amy in so many more ways than only sharing the same height measurement. I mentioned my decades-old jealousy to my mother, and she responded matter-of-factly, "Of course. It was obvious." But not to me.

envying someone's good fortune and coveting their belongings were equivalent in sinfulness.

I didn't say any of those things to Jill.

"I guess I'll have to apologize tomorrow," I said. "But I don't want to be her friend."

When I turned fifteen on Dec. 23, I wanted 1982 to be better than 1981. I promised myself I would be better in every way—physically, emotionally, personally and spiritually. When I thought about the year behind me, I considered myself to be a horrible hypocrite.[12]

I didn't want to tell Amy she had a great tan. Or that she was a great basketball player. Or that she was smarter than I was or skinnier or lucky because she got to go to Florida every year. She was a stinker, but I couldn't hate her. I wanted to be better than that.

When Jill and I parted, I to my house and she to hers, I had two blocks to ponder my situation. It seemed like nothing was going right. January so far had been no better a month than any other. It had been bitterly cold for days. Our basketball team couldn't win a game, and I was no help. I thought maybe I was getting better on defense, but I couldn't make a basket during a game if my life depended on it. I hoped the month would improve, like maybe someone (anyone?) would like me. Because being liked seemed like it would solve all my teenage problems.

I didn't think Brent-the-Cheese liked me. And I *knew* Todd-the-God didn't.

---

[12] If I had been even slightly more forward-thinking, I would have added "socially, intellectually and environmentally" to my laundry list of well-being. I may have acted like a Christian in church, and I may have thought like one, but by my actions and words, people would never know I even *knew* God, and judging by my weekly visits to the Lutheran house of worship, I should have known Him well.

February 24, 1981

Dear Diary,

I got my first proposition today. Brent wanted me to go to bed with him. I think he was joking but he was persistent. Hmm.

February 25, 1981

Dear Diary,

Brent was saying the dirtiest things to me and Jill in social studies today. And some of the meanest, too. It made me feel guilty and insulted at the same time.

February 26, 1981

Dear Diary,

Brent is writing sorta mean songs about me. So I wrote a song about him. But on the last verse I said I liked him. He read it but he was still mean to me.

4

VALERIE STONYRIDGE, Tonya Palomino's basketball practice confidant, moved to Wadena during the summer before seventh grade. In seventh grade, the kids at St. Ann's Catholic school joined the kids who had attended the public elementary school at the Junior High School, so it wasn't strange to see lots of new faces in the hallways. But Valerie was anything but Catholic. She was the type of girl to boldly ask a boy to "go with her" (whatever that meant), and she wouldn't take no for an answer. Her hair was almost white, it was so naturally blonde, and her body was like a rubber band—all taut muscle and energy.

When we were in seventh grade, she formed a group of girls to lip-synch to Queen's "Another One Bites the Dust" during "The Gong Show," the school talent show for Blue & Gold Spirit Week before Homecoming. I was one of the back-up singers lip-synching behind Valerie as she mimed she was "Steve," walking warily down the street with a machine gun ready to go. I remember practicing our dance moves for hours in the basement choir room while Valerie shouted out orders.

"No, you have to move your hands like this, like you're sweeping another one into the dust," she said, adjusting her "Mork & Mindy" rainbow-colored suspenders and then sweeping her hands across her body. "You have to *feel* the music. You have to act out the words."

I had almost no idea what she meant—Wadena was the last place anyone would find a machine gun or bullets ripping out of doorways and I barely grasped the unintelligible lyrics—but I tried to mimic her.

We got gonged by David Green, the mean drummer a year older who locked me in the tiny drum set room one day during Blue Band practice. The talented eighth-grade drummers were in Gold Band with the ninth graders, so David would have been considered second-tier drummer material for having been in the lowly Blue Band that year, and he had the gall to pick up the mallet and hit the enormous dented band gong before we even got to the second verse. What a jerk[13]. But Valerie, ever the confident trail blazer, said, "Keep going, keep going!" and we did until the music screeched to a stop and Mr. O shooed us off the stage.

I admired Valerie for her never-say-die attitude, but she scared me sometimes, too. Maybe she was uncomfortably bold because she lived in a home without a dad, and none of my other friends lived in situations like that. For a girl growing up in a small town with a tight family unit who went to church every week, I didn't have much opportunity to mingle with kids whose parents were divorced. Maybe her parents weren't officially divorced, but her dad was scarce. Valerie never talked about it, but she behaved like she didn't have a

---

[13] David Green *was* a jerk, but in the clarity of hindsight and experience, David Green who locked me in drum set room and gonged my performance had a crush on me. Boys have a weird way of showing interest.

father who would take away her allowance and ground her for two weeks.

In eighth grade, Valerie had a boy-girl party at her house where the infamous Truth, Dare, Double Dare, Promise or Repeat kiss between Craig and me occurred. I don't remember any parents being in the house when dozens of fourteen-year-olds were running amok (my parents would have forbidden my attendance if they knew). When it was my turn to challenge someone, I didn't want anyone to feel as cruddy as I did when Craig kissed me. I posed the query to Bonnie, who was pressed into a corner trying to look invisible.

"Truth, dare, double dare, promise or repeat?" I asked, the words tumbling out of my mouth like machine gun bullets. I concentrated as if I could communicate by telepathy my intentions: *I won't make it hard on you.*

Her eyes ping-ponged in their sockets as she weighed the options: "Truth," she said finally.

"Truth then!" My mind raced as I flailed for an easy question. "Who is your favorite teacher?"

I watched her shoulders relax as she realized I wasn't going to torture her. "Mrs. Cumberland."

Most plays in the game weren't that innocuous, however. Besides the kiss between Craig and I, Valerie and Scott Briller, the tallest boy in our grade—the one who would later surreptitiously cut my hair, went to at least second base. Valerie's willingness to participate enthusiastically struck me as slutty (since pretty much anything beyond passing notes struck me as slutty at the time). I guess it emboldened Scott because then he put an ice cube down my shirt, and I felt sticky for some reason for the rest of the night. But the worst part was when Scott was double-dared to act out the kissing scene on the beach in *From Here to Eternity* with me. Everyone was chanting, "Kiss,

kiss, kiss!" I had never even seen the movie, so I had no idea what he was being double-dared to do. Valerie told me to lie down on the couch, and with everyone in the room, Scott got on top of me and tried to kiss me! I squirmed away so he couldn't plant one. I felt dirty. Valerie just laughed and laughed.

Valerie's boy-girl party had been a fulcrum point in my perspective on boys. Before the truth-or-dare game, I was riding up on the teeter-totter with a thrill in my stomach, viewing boys with interest and reverence; every boy was a potential boyfriend. After the *From Here to Eternity* torture session, I was feeling down with a knot in my stomach; every boy was a potential *fiend*. No longer did I simply want something sweet and vague from them; they wanted something dirty and distinct from me.

Now, a year later, in ninth grade, I was no more sophisticated and Valerie was no less bold. We had study hall instead of choir one day, and Valerie decided to help me flirt with Todd-the-God. She took one of his math papers and held it behind her back.

"Hey, Todd, you want your math paper back?" she said as she waved me behind her.

"Yeah, that would be great," Todd said, his tone betraying his distaste for Valerie as the stupidest person in the room. She clearly wasn't picking up his contempt.

Valerie turned and winked at me, so I grabbed Todd's paper and handed it back to him.

"You're a good kid," he said and flashed me one of his God-like smiles with his dazzling white teeth.

A good *kid*. Todd was a grade younger than I was, and *he* called *me* a kid? But he had also used the adjective *good*. All I could do was smile back. Valerie's eyes bugged out like she was waiting for me to say something, but my tongue was paralyzed. She walked away, shaking her head like I was a hopeless case. But I thought it was kind of Todd to call me *good*.

At that moment, I thought I liked Todd-the-God better than Brent-the-Cheese. I would have loved it if Todd liked me. I would have died of happiness! But I knew better than to think I had a chance with him.

February 11, 1981

Dear Diary,

Craig called tonight and told me to get on the stick. Flirt with Brent or he'll drop me. Ultimatum. I don't know what to do. I am depressed. I want attention. Valerie is telling me that I'm a bitch. Amy is rubbing it in that she is smarter than I am (she got five fewer wrong on the art test). Tonya has a natural talent for getting boys. And I am jealous. I am wasting my time, and I am mad at myself. I am sick and tired of writing in this stupid diary.

Love (hate),
Monica

5

THE WINTER OF 1982 was a cold one. The snow on the ground lost all its moisture and became icy powder. Exposed skin went numb; touching a metal mail box latch or outdoor door knob bordered on painful. School was cancelled on January 15 because of snow. Then it was closed at noon on January 22, and the dance on Saturday, the 23rd, was postponed a week.

"The weather is completely terrible!" I told Jill on the phone during one of the closings. "I am totally bored of it. It's always cold, and that makes the whole world look dreary. The weather is going to be cloudy and snowy and gross again this weekend. Yuck!"

I had apologized to Amy for saying I hated her, but she was pouting. I was learning I couldn't take back my words once I said them. They still stung.[14]

---

[14] Unfortunately, it would take me two decades and one failed marriage to fully learn this lesson. Insults can be forgiven but they aren't forgotten.

On top of everything else, I determined for certain I hated Brent.[15] I had decided, for a day or two anyway, that he was a self-centered, conceited moron.

We had a basketball game against our arch rival, Staples.

It was an adrenaline rush to stand in the hallways outside the gymnasiums at school because just about everyone was there, milling around. *This* is where the action was. The bright lights shined through the glass doorways, beckoning people inside, and the air smelled of cleaning solvent and freshly popped popcorn. I saw Brent-the-Cheese walking down the hallway right behind cute, petite Tonya Palomino on our basketball team. I didn't know if he was talking to her or not, but I butted in.

"Hey, are you coming to our game tonight?" I said.

"No."

No excuses, no feeling, simply "no." He barely looked at me. He simply kept on walking.

I hadn't missed a single one of his games that year and few practices. He should have been grateful. Instead, he was Prince Moron, Duke of Meaninburgh.

Nobody liked me. Not Brent-the-Cheese. Not Todd-the-God. No one, I railed silently to no one in particular. A dance was scheduled for Saturday night, and I knew I wouldn't dance. What a waste of time and money.[16]

Even though I was high scorer with four points, we lost the game to Staples that night, 31-10. I had three air balls in a row at one point

---

[15] Apparently it wasn't OK to hate your best friend, but it was OK to hate the boy you wanted to "go with."

[16] To someone who earned a dollar an hour babysitting other people's cute children, the dance entrance fee of a dollar meant something.

and generally played like a donkey on ice, a typically disappointing performance.

After watching the varsity game, I went to the Pizza Dena with Amy. Todd-the-God was there with Reeve "Mr. Perfect" Koroso's little brother, Royce, and it seemed like Todd was stealing glances at me all night, but it was likely my imagination. He was with a tenth-grade girl who was flirting with him in the bleachers during the varsity game—imagine that! A tenth-grade girl interested in an eighth-grade boy! While we were waiting for our order of French fries to share, Amy said she saw the girl tap him on his butt.

I was sick. *How brash! How dare she!* Of course, I hoped Todd was as wholesome as I was and didn't like it, but he probably did.

The French fries tasted flat and cold after that.

Tonya Palomino was there, too, but she wasn't with Reeve Koroso. She was in a booth with Scott Briller participating in the common practice of PDA: Public Displays of Affection. He had his hand on her thigh, and they were kissing like mad.

"Check that out," Amy said, flipping her hair and crooking her thumb in their direction.

I guess the guys like that stuff, I thought, mentally filing away that tidbit. Sluts get around.

"She'll do anything with anyone," Amy observed.

After we'd devoured our fries, Amy stayed at the Pizza Dena, talking to some admirer or another, but I had to go home to meet MomandDad's curfew. I started trudging towards my house on the snow-covered sidewalks. There was snow everywhere, and even the streets were compacted with slippery white stuff. I was looking down, trying to keep my footing in my plastic-soled blue shoes and move fast through the cold night air.

"Hey, Monica! Whatcha doing?"

I turned around to see Craig Davidson, of the Truth-or-Dare kiss, on his bicycle, a 10-speed. A blue stocking cap with a white stripe covered his red hair, and his cheeks were pink.

"Walking home. What are you doing?" I asked.

"I'm going home, too. You want a ride?" Craig lived another five blocks past my house in a newer split-level house across the street from a park.

"You're crazy," I said. "Why are you riding a bike in the middle of winter? No one does that."

"It works," he shrugged. "Faster than walking."

Craig was trying to be sweet by offering me a ride, and I didn't want to walk. "OK, I'll take a buck on the back. Are you sure about this?"

"Yeah, definitely," Craig said, stepping aside so I could hitch up on the seat of his bike.

Craig stepped back over the bike and prepared to take off.

I didn't know where to put my mittened hands, but I couldn't keep my balance by putting them behind me and the bike on snow was anything but stable. Without other options, I put my hands on his waist while he was putting all his weight on the pedals. He started breathing hard, as the bike picked up speed. I was close enough to smell Craig, and even though he was wearing a winter jacket, he smelled like a combination of pine needles and beach sand.

"So, how's it going?" he said, huffing to catch his breath.

"Fine," I said, noncommittally. "The game sucked tonight. I made four points, but we still lost."

"Can't win all the time," Craig said.

"I know, but it sucks just the same," I said.

We rode in silence for a block.

"Have you heard the new song from Foreigner?" he said.

"No, my favorite song right now is 'No Can Do' by Hall and Oates," I said, thinking of the Billy Joel mix tape he made for me last year. Only it wasn't a mix tape. The only song on it was "It's Still Rock and Roll to Me"—all two minutes and fifty-seven seconds of it, thirteen times over. I must have mentioned I liked that song so he made the tape for me.

"Hall and Oates music is for girls," he said.

"Maybe so," I responded. "I'm a girl."

Pretty soon, we arrived in front of my house.

I scrambled off, trying not to touch him.

"Thanks, Craig," I said, as I hurried to my front door without looking over my shoulder. "You were right! It was faster than walking."

He tries hard, I thought, feeling a tiny bit sorry for him. But I still thought he was gross.

When I stomped in the front door, Dad wasted no time cross examining me. I heard his La-Z-boy clunking to the upright position. "Where were you?" he bellowed.[17] "The game must have been finished more than an hour ago!"

"I went to the Pizza Dena afterward with Amy," I said carefully.

"Who gave you permission for that?" he snorted.

"Dad, it's only ten o'clock," I whined.[18]

---

[17] I have no memories of my father speaking quietly. His hearing was damaged when he operated a jack-hammer in a missile silo in North Dakota for a couple of summers in the early 1960s. He didn't know how loud he spoke—or bellowed if you will—until he got a cochlear implant when I was in my late 40s. In the days after his surgery, he was constantly amazed at how loud everything sounded. Including his own voice.

[18] Dad was and is a stickler for punctuality. He is half German and half Swedish, not Italian (wasn't it Mussolini who's credited for getting the trains to run on time?), but he's rarely late. And that meant I shouldn't be late either.

"I don't care what time it is. I care what you're up to at all hours." I could feel him glaring at me as I walked around him to my bedroom.

"OK, Dad."

February 5, 1981

Dear Diary,

Today during home room, I left to call Valerie from the school office because she was sick. When I came back, Mick, Bob, David and Craig were looking in my folder. Now you know how I love to draw, especially draw women. Well, those guys said I had been drawing dirty pictures. I was more embarrassed than anything but I was angry, too. Literally MAD. Then in study hall, Craig tripped me and I am so mad at him I could spit bricks. I am gonna get him back. Believe you me.

6

BETWEEN HELPING KEEP books for the ninth-grade boys basketball team and actually playing basketball for the girls team, I felt like I did when we were playing Brainerd, whose team tended to play a run-and-gun game up and down the court for four quarters straight: Out of breath.

When the boys played Frazee earlier in the week, I kept score. They lost (again), but I thought they were getting better. When the season began, I promised Brent I'd come to all his games, and he said that if I did, he'd come to mine. At the time, I hoped he'd keep up his end of the deal, but it had gotten embarrassing: We couldn't win either.

When I arrived to get dressed for our game, a friend of Brent's came up to me and said, "Brent likes you!" and then he ran off, like he'd just told the world's funniest joke.

When I walked into the gym, though, Brent didn't say one word to me, so obviously, his friend was lying.

Boys perplexed me. If only they could be like a Rubik's Cube, I could have figured them out. A note I found in my locker after lunch occupied my mind (when I should have been thinking about playing effective defense). The note, written in unfamiliar script, said I liked Craig better and that I was hurting Brent when I sat by Craig in lunch. Hmm. The note wasn't signed. I accused Valerie of writing it, but she vehemently denied it (it wasn't her style to be passive-aggressive anyway), so I thought maybe Jill had penned it. No such luck; she flatly denied having any interest in whom I liked or didn't like. It bugged me that I couldn't figure out who wrote it and how it got into my locker.

My inattention didn't help my performance against Frazee or the team's. We lost 54-3, I dutifully recorded in my diary. It was a long game. "Ugh," I summarized succinctly.

After our game, I sat up in the bleachers to watch the varsity team play. They could actually win sometimes, mostly because of Carrie Williams, the ninth-grade basketball phenom. She got her own smiling picture, cute dimples and all, in the junior high yearbook with the caption: "Girls Varsity Basketball, Carrie Williams." She had the finest hair of any girl in ninth grade, too.

I sat with Amy and Valerie in the stands when Brent walked up the bleachers, two steps at a time.

He sat down next to me. I could feel my heart in my chest, and my face got hot.

"I really hate you," he said like he was ticking off items on a grocery list. "But I like your little sister, Kay. Tell her 'hi' from me and I'll ask her if you did, and if you don't, I'll beat you up."

I looked at him for a second, and he had a sneaky smirk on his face. His green eyes sparkled.

I rolled my eyes. Just then, Carrie scored and the whole crowd cheered. I did, too. I scooted over on the bleachers and pretended to be fascinated with the action on the court.

Brent must have gotten tired of me feigning ignorance because after a while, he left to get some popcorn. When he came back, I was sitting on the bleachers with my knees up and my feet on the seat next to me.

"Move your knees," he ordered. I complied, and he sat down right next to me.

From down the row, Valerie shot me an impressed look.

Though his words were in direct opposition to his actions, I knew Brent knew I liked him because I had written a poem for English class, and Mr. O read it to the seventh-hour class, and I was sure someone in that class told Brent.

This Guy

The boy, his name is Anthony,
He's got it all as you will see.
He's bright, he's tall, he runs real fast,
And in a race, he's never last.

In basketball, he is the best.
He is so smart, he'll ace a test.
But when he looks at me, I'm shy.
And this is why: I like this guy.

Maybe Mr. O thought I simply made it up when he decided to read it aloud to other classes, but he didn't know that Brent's middle name was "Anthony."

+ + +

Once a month or so, the four of us—Amy, Jill, Cindy and I—broke up the monotony of school, sports, church and watching TV with a slumber party. I always had to give a reason—a birthday or a positive report card—for hosting a party, considered an extravagance by my sparing parents, but friends were welcomed warmly overnight at Cindy's house, where we would take over the living room with sleeping bags, pillows and duffle bags filled with sweat suits, slippers and piles of *Seventeen* and *Teen Beat* magazines. Cindy's dad always offered to make Jiffy Pop popcorn on the stovetop,[19] and we would drink pop by the gallon. Soda pop was never stocked at my house; God forbid it would be consumed instead of milk, which built strong bones.

After watching a movie on VHS video[20] or playing a boisterous game of charades, when whatever parents-of-the-house had called it a night and were no longer lurking in the next room, we played slam books.[21]

Here is how it worked: They weren't books, exactly, but single pieces of notebook paper, on which we'd write the names of our friends across the top (so mine said, "Amy," "Jill" and "Cindy"), and then we'd write the categories down the side to create a grid. Usually, categories were "Hair," "Face," "Clothes," "Overall" and "Personality." We passed around the papers and were pressed to write our true and honest opinions in the squares, except only Amy and I seemed to take our mission to heart to improve our friends with our unvarnished opinions.

The weekend after the poetry reading in English class, Cindy hosted a slumber party with all the signature elements: Sleeping bags,

---

[19] Microwave popcorn was still the stuff of dreams by future forecasters.
[20] Betamax was so last year.
[21] Slam books were the 1982 equivalent of "Do You Think I'm Pretty" YouTube videos.

popcorn, a viewing of *Friday the 13th* on the console TV in the living room and, of course, slam books.

When the slam books returned to their owners, the quiet of pencils scribbling on paper was replaced by the quiet of teenage girls taking in their friends' opinions.

Here's how mine looked:

Hair

Amy: It looks nice tonight. I've got to tell you, you look better now than in your sixth-grade picture.

Jill: "LOVE IT!" with a bunch of stars drawn around the words.

Cindy: Looks very nice *all* the time.

Face

Amy: Personally, I think you need more or darker blush to make your cheekbones stick out.

Jill: Your makeup looks nice and natural to me! Try what Amy says and if I hate it, I'll let you know. Or vice versa.

Cindy: Very nice work on make-up. Maybe you could work on your cheek bones coming out more.

Clothes:

Amy: You've added a lot of variety to your wardrobe this year.

Jill: Monique's Boutique—MMM! Yummy!

Cindy: Always fit nice. You wear all your clothes well.

Overall

Amy: I don't know of anything that's wrong. Even though Scott Briller says you have an underbite, I don't think it's noticeable.

Jill: Fine with me! Us pals gotta stick together.

Cindy: Your personality is much better, and you're more considerate.

Personality

Amy: You act weird at times. Sometimes I get hyper about it because I think it's unnecessary but that's my problem.

Jill: Weird people are the best!! You are getting better in this department! Sometimes I feel overpowered but this *rarely* happens.

Cindy: Your personality is much better than last year. Not as many rude comments and criticism.

I savored reading Jill's droll comments. I wasn't intuitive enough to know she was as politically correct as she was witty. I knew exactly what Amy meant by calling me "weird." She meant "mean." I knew she was right. But why did she have to tell me that Scott Briller thought I had an underbite?

As in life, Cindy was polite on paper, but she had me thinking about my critical nature. I thought I was only being honest. Thou shalt not bear false witness against thy neighbor, right?[22]

---

[22] I hadn't yet learned honesty and kindness were not mutually exclusive.

January 13, 1981

Dear Diary,

Today I cheated in English. I gave my spelling paper to Phil, Ron, David and some other boys. Mrs. Cumberland walked by and saw them. Everyone involved got in trouble. Ohhh my.

January 14, 1981

Dear Diary,

Today Mrs. Cumberland said that she didn't flunk me but she flunked everyone else involved. Yesterday I got a real scare on that. My room is right above the family room and whatever you say down there can be heard up in my room. Well, last night I heard words like "copying," "copying from her paper" and stuff. I was in bed and I froze. Today I asked my mom "Did Mrs. Cumberland call you?" Mom said, "No, why? Should she have?" "Oh no, I just wondered." I made up that excuse pretty fast.

7

BRENT DEFINITELY KNEW about the poem and so did everyone else in school.

It was the Friday before Valentine's Day, and it began auspiciously. My little brother, Curtis, who was in third grade, gave me a homemade Valentine at breakfast. On the front, he wrote in block print:

> Happy Valentines Monica. Be mine. I love you.

Inside, it read:

> Roses are red,
> violas are blue,
> I love you,
> hope you love me.
> Love Curtis

Only he had crossed out "violas" and wrote "violets." His poetry was like his jokes: Not quite finished. He had learned to appreciate poetry and humor from our grandfather, but he hadn't yet learned the finer points. Just the *way* he told a joke was the funniest part. As he told the joke, the suspense wasn't in the punch line but whether he would have one or, if he did, how he would botch it.

"Knock, knock."

"Who's there?"

"Three pigs."

"Three pigs who?"

"Knock knock."

"What? I don't get it," I'd say. "'Knock knock' is the pigs' last name? That doesn't make sense."

"They're knocking. That's the joke. They're not ringing the doorbell."

"Oh, Curt, they're not ringing the doorbell. *That's* the joke. The last line should be 'Three pigs who can't reach the doorbell.'"

"Oh." And then he would laugh like it was the funniest joke he'd ever told.

I had decided Curtis was my favorite family member in the house. Mom and Dad were always picking on me, at least that's what I believed, and Kay was always tattling on me or performing some other form of mean retribution for perceived slights. Just the other day, she said loudly, in front of Mom, that I was sleeping with K.C., our Siamese cat, which I was not supposed to do. I knew Mom must have heard her, but she didn't say anything, which surprised me. Most of the time, I hated my parents, like, HATE with capital letters. All MomandDad ever did was put restrictions on me. Then they expected me to be happy with lots of rules and to behave cordially. When I didn't, they yelled and cracked down even more. I hated them. I would have killed myself but I wanted to live just to punish them.

Curtis, on the other hand, with his sincere blue eyes and practically colorless straw hair was always affectionate. Plus, I got paid when I babysat him.

One Sunday, the most boring day of the week, I took a nap in the afternoon because I stayed out late the night before to see the movie *Raiders of the Lost Ark* with Cindy and Valerie. The best part of the evening wasn't the movie; it was that we saw the tenth grader who touched Todd-the-God's butt at the Pizza Dena. But we didn't see Todd. So they weren't an item after all. Because we always watched reruns together on Sunday afternoons, Curt woke me up from my nap in time to watch *Wonder Woman*. We were TV fanatics. When I didn't have basketball, we also watched *The Incredible Hulk* and *The Dukes of Hazzard* on Friday nights.

It was kind of him to give me a Valentine. Kay didn't. She did tell me I wrote good poems though.

When I got to school, Jill and I made posters that said, "Good luck, Guys" for the eighth and ninth grade boys basketball teams for their games against Staples, and that made me happy, too. But during first period, Amy told me she heard Brent say (with a smile on his face) that he wished I would just leave him alone. Besides the message, she gave me a carnation, too, with a note that said, "Friends forever."

Valentines from brothers and friends were pleasant, but Brent's message via Amy was just plain mean. I was feeling low in general business class.

"What's your problem?" Valerie asked.

"I don't know," I said, drawing circles on my profit-and-loss worksheet. "Brent told Amy he wishes I would just leave him alone."

"I have him in math next period. I'll ask him if he likes you."

"You would? That would be great," I said.

When I saw Valerie in the hallway after math, she gave me an uncomfortable look.

"Well?"

"I talked to him, but I can't tell you," she said, like she had a terrible secret.

"C'mon, tell me," I pleaded.

"Can't," she said and turned to stack her books in her locker.

After band, I walked into the lunchroom looking for Jill and Amy and Cindy.

"Hey, happy Valentine's Day!" I said, pointing to the heart-shaped sugar cookies we got for dessert.

"Yuck," Amy said, nibbling on her granola bar.

"Valerie told me something awful today," Cindy said.

We all perked up, leaning over our food to hear the gossip.

"What?" Jill said.

"She said she's trying to kill herself," Cindy said, her eyes wide. "She says she's not eating until Scott Briller likes her."

"How sick," I said.

"And he doesn't even know," Cindy said.

"Wow," Amy said, like she was thinking it over as a tactic she might use.

"That's stupid," Jill said, pushing her tray away from her. "I'm done."

I was done, too, and as we were about to get up, student council representatives started handing out pocket-sized pink pieces of paper. Somebody gave me one. On one side, it said "Coupon! Coupon! See other side!" My stomach flipped. On the other side, it said, "This coupon is redeemable for one hug from any participating human being! P.S. There is no expiration date! P.P.S. I love you!"

It was signed with Craig Davidson's name.

Ugh.

I stuffed it in my back pocket and headed for the garbage cans with my lunch tray.

I meant to corner Valerie on the bus to Aitken for our game and try to extract information from her about Brent, but she didn't go. We lost 54-13. I made one point.

We got back in time for the last twenty minutes of the Valentine's Day dance. Dances for the Junior High School were held in the cafeteria. All the fold-up tables with their attached, round, plastic seats were pushed to the sides of the room, and a deejay set up his music and lights on the foot-high stage in the front of the room. Sometimes, somebody hung streamers and painted signs, but typically the only decoration was a disco ball hanging from the ceiling.

The first person I tracked down was Valerie.

"Seriously, what did he say?" I said without even telling her our team had lost again.

"I don't want to be the one to tell you," Valerie said.

But I had heard she told her friend, Bonnie, the meek girl from Carrie's eighth grade truth-or-dare party, so I asked her. "He likes you, OK, but he swore Valerie to secrecy, OK?" Bonnie said.

So I was truly happy for about one minute. Then I talked to Mick Bierbrauer, my friend from church confirmation class, who had no regard for junior high social mores and was standing with Craig on the girls' side of the cafeteria. Mick leaned over (or perhaps it was more like leaning up) and conspiratorially told me Brent danced with my sister Kay and her friend before I got there. My heart swelled like it had been punched, and my throat closed.

The last song at dances was always a slow song, and this dance was no different. At the end, the first strains of "Beth" by KISS started playing. I didn't like KISS, but I thought "Beth" was romantic and it had the ideal beat for a couple to sway together slowly and dreamily.

Brent walked over to where we all were standing. I assumed he was coming to ask me to dance so I held my breath and looked nonchalantly out on to the dance floor.

He walked past me and said to Valerie, "Wanna dance?" She flounced out onto the dance floor with him, he put his hands on her hips, and she draped her arms on his shoulders.

What?!

"We're outta here. Come on," I said aloud to Amy. And I marched out of the cafeteria.

"I wonder if Brent was trying to make me jealous?" I said to Amy as we walked home. "Maybe he actually does like me."

"Listening to your boy fantasies gets boring sometimes," Amy said.

I trudged along the sidewalk in silence, thinking about the dance. Todd Byrd and the tenth grader unquestionably were going together. He didn't even come to the dance.

But they didn't bother me. It was Brent. If Brent liked me, he certainly wasn't showing it. He probably didn't like me, which was a total bummer.

"Next week is spirit week," I said. "What are you wearing for '50s Day on Monday?"

"I have a circle skirt with a poodle on it," Amy said, plowing into a complete description of every piece of clothing she was wearing on Monday, her makeup and how she was going to do her hair, barely taking a breath between each dramatic element of her ensemble. I muttered appropriate expressions of "cool" and "uh-huh," but I was thinking about Slave Day, which was on Thursday. Slave Day was a fund-raiser for the student council, when members were auctioned into indentured servitude to the highest bidder.[23] I had a choice between buying Todd-the-God or Brent-the-Cheese. As Amy debated the relative merits of green or blue eye shadow with herself, I wondered which potential boyfriend I should invest in: One who liked having his butt tapped by tenth graders or one who professed to hate me.

---

[23] If this tradition was an attempt by some history teacher to illuminate the tragic, disrespectful and exploitive nature of measuring the value of human beings in dollars in nineteenth century slave auctions, it eluded me in 1982. I just wanted to order someone around, preferably someone in whom I had a romantic interest.

February 10, 1981

Dear Diary,

I went to a basketball game tonight with Amy and Cindy. Tonya was there, too. We saw these cute guys from Fergus Falls (that's who we played). They were in ninth grade. Their names were Nick, Chris, Rod and Steve. I like Chris. Nick was cute, too. But guess who asked Tonya to go into the locker room. You got it. Mine. Chris. I also liked Nick but so did Amy. Oh well. Maybe I can find out their addresses.

8

BUTCHER-PAPER POSTERS for each member of student council were taped on the wall outside the library on the third floor of the Junior High School, right around the corner from my locker so I could keep an eye on the auction bids for Todd-the-God and Brent-the-Cheese. Scott Briller was too cool to be a member of student council or I might have considered buying him.

Todd-the-God was out of my budget by second period. A group of girls in eighth grade pooled their money, and the bid rocketed as high as one of Todd's jump shots. But I was leading with Brent, and I had already planned to have him clean my locker as my slave. I was going to get my money's worth. Bids were supposed to be final at the beginning of lunch period.

It was Punk Day for spirit week. I dressed like Debbie Harry from Blondie, and I wore my Gitano jeans though there was some question about that as I got dressed for school that morning. They were so tight, I had to lie on the bed to zip them up; the scene caught my Dad's eye as he passed my bedroom. "What are you *doing?!*" If Debbie Harry had had a butt of glass instead of a heart of glass, it would have been crushed under the pressure. As confused about what defined "punk" as I had been when I wore an Army green shirt to impress Scott Briller, I also believed "punk" meant a ton of eye makeup and hairspray, which I had layered on with a putty knife and a garden hose. All this was to impress Brent and acquire him as my slave. I hoped *he* liked it.

Brent was mine when Mr. O took the posters down, but somehow, inexplicably, Tonya Palomino ended up outbidding me by one cent.

One lousy cent.

By a cheater.

Who was Tonya Palomino anyway? She with her long hair was a cute, diminutive baton twirler in band prancing around like a fairy granting her own wishes, but her most sizeable talent was flirting. With Brent, apparently. Who knows what else she was doing with him. I didn't like to think about it.

"How did you get Brent for your slave?" Amy cornered Tonya at lunch for me. Amy looked tough compared to petite Tonya, but Tonya was like a coiled spring.

"Um, I bid the most. That's how it works," Tonya said and pranced away with Brent in tow, carrying her lunch tray.

Brent didn't say anything.

I seethed. Like it did me any good.

On top of my big hair and unrealized dreams of slave ownership, I got an 88 on my test in math. For most people, this would be awesome. For me, it was failure. I would almost certainly get a B for the quarter, I was sure of it. If I did, I would just die. I'd die. In the most dramatic way possible.

While I slumped in my desk, chewing on what an 88 meant to my grade, I noticed Craig eyeing me. His red hair was dyed black, and he was wearing a studded dog collar with a black leather vest over a white T-shirt. He had captured the punk ethos better than I had.

"I dreamed about you last night," he said.

Oh, great, I thought. I looked away.

"I don't want the details," I said, feeling flushed.

The only positive of the day was gym, the class I normally hated the most. We were doing the square dancing unit—an ironic foil for punk aspirations—and Ike O'Trell asked me to be his partner. He held my hand as we moved through our do-si-dos. He was cute and polite but kind of quiet and he had no idea he should be feathering his hair. I was just glad he picked me. It's all that mattered—*he* picked *me*. So I found him appealing.

A few days later, Shelley Anson celebrated her birthday, and Brent-the-Cheese gave her a card. He had never given *me* a card.

Hold on, Brent was dancing with Valerie at the Valentine's dance, yesterday he was following Tonya's orders, and today he was sucking up to Shelley Anson. Keeping track of his whims was almost as complicated as keeping track of my own. Why Shelley now? Why did he like *her*?

Shelley was voted Class Duchess at Homecoming last fall, and she had flawless skin, wavy dark brown hair and slow-blinking doe eyes. And she wasn't loud, like I was. She was sweet, and she could have anyone she wanted. She even *knew* I liked him. I guess everyone did, though. That was the drawback to being inappropriately loud. I found it grotesque—not simply gross, but the full-blown *grotesque*—that Brent liked her. It made my stomach turn. Why her? Brent liked girls who flirted outrageously, like Tonya Palomino or Shelley Anson, likely because he didn't like to take the initiative, I decided.

If that was what he wanted, Brent-the-Cheese was someone I didn't need to be interested in. Screw him.

I felt alone and unwanted. And I imagined I would do anything to feel differently, only I knew I wouldn't do *anything*. I wouldn't take the initiative and ask a boy to dance. I wouldn't lie on the couch and reenact a kissing scene. And I certainly wouldn't blow on a guy's dick.

Scott Briller had been saying "Hi" to me and making conversation in science class, instead of surreptitiously cutting my hair to get my attention. Maybe I liked him, I decided. Or maybe Ike O'Trell, my square-dance partner.

"I heard there's going to be a dance for St. Patrick's Day," Cindy said at lunch with the four of us in the Hamster Cage.

"Well, I doubt if I'm going to go," I said, thinking of the Valentine's Day dance disaster. "Why waste the money?"

"I'll borrow you a dollar," Amy said.

"Maybe we could walk around town and maybe just visit the dance every once in a while," I said hopefully.

"Count me out," Jill said.

"What's the use? I never dance anyway," I said.

"Neither do I," Cindy said.

That didn't make me feel better. Cindy hadn't even been kissed yet. At least I had been kissed by a boy, even though it was on a dare.

I figured I would end up going to the dance anyway even though I expected to sit on the sidelines all night. I didn't want to sit at home, either.

Dateline: 1/30/82

Dear Diary,

I am totally sick! It's not fair! It's not fair! Todd-the-God asked Shay to dance—first a fast, then a slow! I'm just sick! Sick! Sick! Why can't I be happy? There's got to be something wrong with me! Why her! It's not fair! I'm just as pretty as she is! Aren't I? I wanna die! I wanna die! I wanna die! I wanna die! Die! Die!

9

I HOPED EVERYTHING would look brighter in the spring, but so far, not even the robins were stupid enough to make an appearance. It wasn't even warm enough to rain. It was 10 below zero on March 1, and then we got two inches of snow. At church, we were observing Lenten season, which meant going to midweek services every Wednesday night. Hearing about betrayals and slaves getting their ears cut off and crucifixions didn't make my spirits brighter.

I guessed I was having emotional problems.[24] I had written two poems and a story about suicide, and I wondered if that was an ominous sign.

The dance I had been alternately looking forward to and dreading for two weeks finally arrived. Mom agreed to French braid my hair

---

[24] Surely hormones had nothing to do with my moods, I might have said with sarcasm if I had had more experience with hormones. As I wrangle with menopause in my 40s (and my hormones fluctuate widely once again), I realize hormones influence my mood, my appetite, my arousal, my energy level, my ability to sleep deeply, my attitude about my reflection in the mirror and just about everything else that might dictate my self-esteem and ability to work and play well with others. No wonder I was constantly swinging between "I want a boyfriend" and "I want to die."

for the dance. I was hoping for a moment I could classify as "the best of March" in my diary. My long-debated ensemble consisted of Sassoon jeans and the green-and-white crew neck sweater I had just finished knitting. I was pleased at my second attempt at knitting a sweater.

"Your sweater looks fashionable," Mom remarked as she parted my hair.

"Yeah, better than the first one I made," I said. Setting in sleeves was a complex knitting procedure I hadn't mastered with my first sweater, and I looked like a football player when I wore it because the shoulders were oversized. The green-and-white sweater had a pattern across my barely burgeoning chest, and it was white by my face, which I hoped made me look tanner.

"Looking forward to the dance?" Mom asked as she braided.

"Yeah, I hope Todd Byrd asks me to dance," I said. "He's so cute."

"So I've heard," Mom said.

I had heard the tenth grader who touched his butt at the Pizza Dena didn't like Todd. I was hoping against hope that might be good news for me.

"But he probably won't ask me. He probably thinks I'm a dork."

"Well, then that would be his loss," Mom said.

"I wish someone liked me," I said.

"Lots of people like you," Mom said. "Amy likes you, Jill likes you, Cindy likes you."

"I don't mean girls. I mean boys."

"Seems like Craig likes you."

"He doesn't count," I sighed. "I wish somebody I *like* liked me."

Mom secured one braid and started working on the hair on the other side of my head.

"Well, it doesn't always work out the way we think it should," Mom said. "Try to keep an open mind, and you'll have fun no matter who asks you to dance."

"If *anyone* asks me," I said. "I just hope they're tall."

"Is that how you judge boys, by how tall they are?"

"Yeah," I said, like she'd never looked at the daughter who towered inches over her 5-foot-3 frame. *"I'm* tall."

"How about looking at how smart he is? Or considerate? Or if he makes you laugh? Or if he's a good kisser?"

"Yuck. Don't talk about that," I said.

"There's more to a man than what you can measure with a yardstick,"[25] she said as she secured the other braid. "There, what do you think?"

"I love it," I said looking into the hand mirror as I tucked her piece of advice in the back of my mind, not wanting to discuss it with her. "It's perfect. Thanks!"

Nominated for carpool, Dad picked up Jill and Amy and dropped all of us off in front of the cafeteria doors.

"Be good," he said, as we scrambled out of his baby blue Ford Crown Victoria.

"Bye, Dad," I said.

We walked down the hallway to the darkened cafeteria, standing in the doorway while our eyes adjusted to the lack of light. Most of the boys were on the right side, and most of the girls were on the left. A knot of teachers and chaperones stood in the back, surveying the scene. The music pulsed, but no one was dancing.

"Ooh. This looks like fun," Jill deadpanned.

---

[25] My mother, whom I adore, has carried her skill for being nonjudgmental and supportive in matters of the heart into our adult relationship.

We ambled in and joined the girls' side.

By the end of the night, it was clear my new sweater wasn't a good luck charm. Brent wasn't there at all. I danced four times, most of them with less-than-thrilling boys in my grade—one of them was fat, one of them was short and one of them was a member of Future Farmers of America, which was not my scene. I didn't mean to besmirch the profession of farming (or fat boys or short ones for that matter). I had two grandfathers who were farmers, and I now understand the importance of their work in the grand scheme of my diet, but my experience with agriculture at that point was limited to spending time on my maternal grandfather's farm in western North Dakota, a lonely claim on a windswept hill filled with junk. My exposure to farming at that point in my life was defined by witnessing my father tinker with my grandfather's rusty farm implements and the enormity of the bowel movements of the cows my grandfather milked. I wasn't impressed.

The fourth dance was with Scott Briller. Of the four dancing encounters, the only memorable one was with Scott, and I asked *him*. We danced next to Todd-the-God and some other girl, and that was almost as good as dancing with Todd.

But the night ended up being more than just disappointing. The girl who had tapped Todd-the-God on the butt at the Pizza Dena was there. Since she was in tenth grade, she wasn't supposed to be at a junior high dance, but nobody kicked her out (which irked the rule-following oldest daughter in me). She didn't dance, which was fine with me, until the last two dances. She and Todd stood together most of the night, their heads bent towards each other like they were whispering the world's best secrets. Apparently, she had talked to Todd long enough to brainwash him, and *he* asked *her* to dance—first a fast one, then a slow dance.

I was heartsick. She liked Todd, and I just knew he liked her. She had a whole school of tenth graders to choose from, and she went for an eighth grader. It just wasn't fair in my fifteen-year-old eyes.

I slept over at Jill's after the dance, a reward for not talking back to my parents all week. We broke into a bag of Old Dutch Rip-L-Chips and dunked them repeatedly in French onion dip while sipping cans of Diet Coke.

"Well, that was lame," Jill said of the dance. "I don't think St. Patrick would be proud."

"It sucked," I agreed. "I'm never gonna get a boyfriend."

"You couldn't date him even if you got 'im," she said, fully briefed on my parents' no-dating-until-sixteen dictate.

After we finally turned out the lights in the wee hours of the morning, I snuggled in my sleeping bag and thought about the year so far and boys and my friends.[26] I thought about the promises I made to myself on my birthday—nearly three months before—to be a better person. How often had I said I should be more considerate of my friends, and then reverted to harsh words and cold shoulders? Lying there in the dark of Jill's basement family room, I decided yet again, from now on, I would try harder.

I knew myself to be notorious about embracing a *tabula rasa*. I started diets, new exercise programs and better habits on "new days": Mondays, the first day of a month or the beginning of the year. Even at fifteen, I was a New Year's resolution addict.[27]

---

[26] Because when you're a fifteen-year-old girl, life does not exist without boys and friends.

[27] I still make New Year's Resolutions every year, and now they even have themes. In 2015, I resolved to "savor adventure" by being my own best friend and savoring time by being present in the moment and listening actively. Also, to read more books.

I was going to start the fourth quarter of ninth grade as a new person. I guessed tenth grade class elections were held in the spring of ninth grade so if I wanted to win, I figured I had to be friendlier. To everyone. Or at least quieter. That would be my goal: To be on student council next year. Student council members were voted to the position by everyone else in the class. I wondered if I could reach that goal.

And I made another, seemingly more important goal. Since I was allowed to date when I turned sixteen, I needed a boyfriend by then. I must find someone to like me. I had less than nine months, which seemed like an impossibly long duration and a blink at the same time. I decided I had the beginning of a new month to start with a clean slate. "I'm going to stick by my contract," I wrote in my diary the next night. "I *want* to change."

The following Monday during Mr. Bandicot's history class, I watched my friend Mick take notes in his microscopic writing in the corner of a sheet of notepaper.

"Why are you writing so small?" I whispered across his desk. I admired Mick's high I.Q. and his ability to memorize Bible verses after reading them once, but I also thought he was a bit strange.

"I'm going to try to get all my notes this quarter on one piece of paper," he said, concentrating on his tiny print.

"How can you even read that?"

He looked up, staring at me like he couldn't understand how my simple brain worked. "I like a challenge."

I raised my eyebrows and pursed my lips. "OK then." I pulled a sheet of narrow-ruled notepaper out of my Trapper Keeper and began writing *A Novel Idea* in my third-grade-perfect cursive handwriting, admiring my script as much as my words as I wrote. My high-concept story was as novel an idea as its title: A progressive story written by me and my friends—not just a short story, a *book*. Mick could have his single sheet of history notes at the end of the quarter; I wanted something more substantial. I penned the first line: "Gwendolyn Joy Hayes: Old maid in tenth grade" and proceeded to write a semi-autobiographical description of Gwendolyn's love life. By inviting Amy, Jill and Cindy to help write the story, I fancied that *A Novel Idea* would be a way to bond with my friends and exert some control over something in my life. The characters in my real life weren't so easy to manage.

January 13, 1981

Dear Diary,

I am starting to write a novel. It's a love story-mystery wrapped into one. Hmm.

January 15, 1981

Dear Diary,

Today in shop I playfully threw a ruler at Craig, and I hit him in the eye. I felt bad. He looked like he was going to cry. I said "sorry" a couple of times but I still felt like a glass of wine at an AA meeting. So dumb. (Sigh!)

P.S. I quit the novel.

10

"HERE, YOUR TURN," I said as I shoved a pile of notebook paper tied in the margin holes with blue yarn into Amy's tan hands during the five-minute break between history and English.

"What's this?"

"It's the beginning of a story," I said. "We're going to pass it around and write it together. I started it, you can add something to the story, then Cindy, and then Jill. I composed it in history during another one of those 'You Are There' movies that Mr. Bandicot thinks are worth watching."

"OK," she said, trying to please me. She could tell I was irked with her. She glanced at the first line of *A Novel Idea*. "Gwendolyn Joy Hayes, huh? That's an interesting name for a main character."

"I made it up," I said. "I think it's cool. Get it? 'Joy'?"

"Joy is the middle name," she said. "What's there to get?"

"Don't be dense. It's metaphor."

"Right. Metaphor," she nodded. Amy was bright enough to know what "metaphor" meant, but she had no idea why I thought that was relevant. I wasn't sure I did, either. She didn't give anything away, though. "So, what do you want me to write?"

"Whatever you want to write," I said. "I'm sure you'll come up with something brilliant. Pass it on to Cindy when you're done, and then she can give it to Jill, and then Jill can give it back to me."

+ + +

District playoffs in basketball had started. Janet Karvonen, the state's greatest girls basketball player with the perfect jump-shot, had graduated and wasn't playing for New York Mills anymore, but the team was still good, and Mills beat Staples in the first round. Carrie Williams and Wadena's varsity team would get its chance against Mills next, and I just hoped there would be a student bus to see the game. We just *had* to win or at least that's how I felt at the time, pinning much of my self-esteem onto teams that carried the Wadena name even if I had nothing whatsoever to do with the team other than the shared blue-and-gold uniform.

The last game for the ninth-grade girls had been the previous week against Park Rapids. I had the chance to make a Janet-Karvonen-perfect jump-shot, and I missed. But I made two of four free throws, which amounted to an astounding success ratio for me. My record for the year was fifteen fouls and nineteen points, as I carefully recorded in my diary. At the time, I thought that wasn't too shabby considering our team never made more than sixteen points in a game. I'm sure my frequent fouls were less strategic and more expressions of frustration.[28]

---

[28] As I consider my short and unremarkable basketball career (I quit after the season in eleventh grade, unwilling to warm the bench as a senior), I realize I never fulfilled the promise I might have shown at the beginning. I was tall and smart; even in all my seventh-grade gawkiness, a coach might have seen potential. But I lacked the resilience necessary to persevere

Brent-the-Cheese was there, watching our last game. I was sure he wasn't impressed, but he had no right to think he was better than I was. The last game I saw him play, he missed six free throws in a row. I felt sorry for him.

I still liked Brent. I had hardly even glanced at Todd-the-God lately. Todd and the tenth grader broke up, and I cheered when I heard, but I also declared I didn't care.[29]

Finally, it was the girls varsity basketball team's turn to take on New York Mills in the district playoffs, and I climbed onto the student fan bus filled with hope and optimism. Our team was ahead by eight points at half-time, and it was an excitingly close game until the end of the fourth quarter. Amy, Jill, Valerie and I jumped around like crazy on the bleachers, which were packed to the ceiling. It was so loud in the gym, I could hardly hear myself yell. But the varsity girls lost by four points. I remember being bummed out for twenty-four hours until the boys varsity team beat Backus in their district game by one point with a free throw in the last four seconds. My diary fails to record how the boys team did in their next game, which leads me to believe they lost so miserably I couldn't even bear to record it.

One Saturday afternoon, I curled up on the blue sofa Dad constructed from plywood and upholstery fabric for the basement, writing a poem and watching a rerun of "In Search of ...." Narrator

---

through failure; if it was hard (and "killers" were hard), I wanted to quit and frequently checked out. Unlike schoolwork, which came easily to me, physical exertion required a tolerance for discomfort that I didn't have. Losing game after game on top of the daily physical grind did nothing to stoke the fire in my belly for basketball.

[29] Just as the lack of success on the basketball court strangled my enthusiasm for the sport, Todd's obliviousness to my crush made me want to fold.

Leonard Nimoy's voice distracted me from my rhymes: "This series presents information based in part on theory and conjecture. The producer's purpose is to suggest some possible explanations, but not necessarily the only ones, to the mysteries we will examine."

About halfway into the mystery of a detective who used extra-sensory perception to fight crime, Mom's footsteps clicked down the stairs.

"Here are your drum sticks," she said handing them to me.

"Where did you get these?" I asked.

"Craig just came to the door and gave them to me. He told me to give them to you," Mom said, walking off to throw another load of clothes into the washing machine in the utility room next door. I twirled the sticks with my fingers, wondering how Craig got his hands on them.

I walked to Amy's house for dinner later, and Craig—ever willing to endure crappy Minnesota weather no matter what the season—rode by on his bike.

"Hey! Where did you get my drum sticks?" I asked, as he slowed down to my speed.

"Oh, you got them back?" he said.

"Yeah, Mom gave them to me," I said. "Thanks. Where did you find them?"

"I dunno," he shrugged. "Someone must have put them in my trombone case during band."

"OK, that's weird," I said, thinking about how the trombone players sat on the other side of the room from the drummers.

"Yeah, I thought so, too," he said. "Whatcha doing tonight?"

"Amy and I are going to the movies," I said. Craig made small talk until I got to the sidewalk in front of Amy's house. "Bye," I said, and Craig rode off.

When I got inside, I learned Cindy was going to the movies with us. And so was Craig. Craig had only agreed to go if he could sit by me, Cindy told me, and Cindy agreed if she could sit on his other side. So Craig knew exactly what I was doing when he asked "Whatcha doing?"

"Do you like Craig?" I asked Cindy.

"No," Cindy said, biting her fingernails. "He wanted to sit by you."

After the movie, "Swamp Thing," which was a story without a point, Craig rode off on his bike as usual, and Amy, Cindy and I walked back to Amy's house for ice cream. As I was leaving to go home, I walked out the front door by myself and Craig stood like a statue with wide eyes on the doorstep. Instantly, my heart was racing faster than a Journey song, and my hands got sweaty. "You scared me! I hate you!" I screamed as I pushed past him and stomped down the sidewalk.

He hopped on his bike and rode away without comment.

"It's done!" I muttered under my breath. "Over. I do *not* like Craig. I have no feelings in my heart for him *at all.*" Apparently, admonishing myself was somehow necessary.

+ + +

Since basketball season was over for me, Mom and Dad insisted I take swimming lessons. I had been swimming and taking lessons at Wadena's outdoor municipal pool for years, during which I spent summer afternoons paddling around so long I ended up wrinkled and waterlogged, but these newly scheduled lessons were at the indoor Olympic-sized pool in Staples, twenty miles away. Upon completion, I would earn my water safety instructor certification so that I could be a lifeguard, but I didn't even want to be a lifeguard. I would have to wear a swimsuit all day, and boys would ogle me. MomandDad, however, was thinking of my future job options even if I wasn't.

Amy took lessons with me. We didn't know anyone else in the class, and most of the others were boys.

Almost immediately, Amy decided she was in love with one of the assistant lifesaving instructors. He had sandy blond hair on his head and none on his chest. I thought it looked weird.[30] I also thought Amy's fantasy was only a pipe dream. She would never get far with an older guy from a different town.

I was the slowest swimmer[31] in the pool which embarrassed me with every stroke. I thought I risked flunking so it would be a waste of time anyway. "If you can't be the best, don't bother even trying" was my motto. But my swimming performance was the least of my worries in the pool. I fretted I was going to get my period on Tuesday, the day we had swimming lessons. My stomach hurt and my hands got sweaty just thinking about it. I couldn't use tampons—way too scary—and I knew other girls went to lessons with their periods. *I would just die,* I wrote in my diary. *But what can I do except pray?*

---

[30] I have since learned swimmers shave their body hair so they have less resistance in the water, shaving tenths of a second off their swim times.

[31] Maybe I could have used a shave.

April 3, 1981

Dear Diary,

I had a dream last night (this morning?) about being on a bike trip with Pam, Cindy and Amy, and I thought it was such as good plan that I told everybody in school about it and they liked it. A lot. So we decided where we would go for a week on our bikes. I talked to Mom and Dad about it and they said I should try a one night trip first and if that works out ... well, maybe. Oh, I can't wait 'til June. It will be so fun.

Love, Monica

11

"Really, Jill?" I said into the phone. "A clarinet-banjo duet?"

"Hey, it was your idea to write a collaborative story," Jill said. "I thought it was funny. It made me laugh. Didn't you laugh?"

It was Wednesday evening. No swimming lessons. Supper was done. Homework was done. And I had a half hour before having to go to choir practice with Mom at church. So I was sitting in the hallway between my bedroom and my sister's, twirling my hair in my fingers and talking on the phone with Jill about *A Novel Idea* and her less-than-novel plot twists.

"I guess I'll have to figure something out," I said, ignoring her question.

"So, when are you going to get your ears pierced?" Jill asked. My parents had finally relented and agreed to let me pierce my ears as long as I paid for it. I had the money; now I was working up the courage.

"I could do it Friday," I said. "Want to go with me?" Amy and Jill had pierced their ears long ago, but Jill tore hers when she caught her hoops in her sweater and had to let the holes grow shut.

"After school? That works," she said. "I'll get mine re-pierced at the same time."

"I'm sooo scared that it will hurt."

"It doesn't hurt. Don't be such a baby. It's worth the pain."

"Do we have to make an appointment at the clinic?"

"Clinic? No way. You act like it's major surgery. It's cheaper if we go to the tech school."

Jill was right, as she typically was. We waited in line longer at the cosmetology department at the technical school than it actually took to punch holes in our ears. The pain was sharp at first, and then a numb ache for about as long as it took to walk home; then I just spent my time admiring the shiny silver studs in my ears. I loved them. In my mind, adults pierced their ears so my pierced ears meant I was an adult. Or closer to one, anyway.

April began with a kick in the mouth and a report card filled with straight A grades. For the report card, Dad gave me $5. For the kick in the mouth, I got an imperfect smile that lasted twenty years.

My little brother practiced cart wheels in the living room, and for once I was trying to be a helpful big sister. I stood on the side of the projected wheel rut, guiding his feet over the top of his body as he turned. Curtis was about as coordinated as I was, which is to say, not very. My face got in the way of his cart-wheeling foot and whack! Down I went.

"Ouch!" I yelled, holding my face. If I thought getting my ears pierced would hurt, I didn't count on the pain of getting kicked in the face.

"Oh, I'm so sorry!" My meek little brother's face was crumpled. "I didn't mean to."

"OK, we're done practicing cartwheels," I said, nursing my wounds.

I looked in the mirror inspecting the damage, and I appeared to have survived mostly unscathed. The blood was from a cut lip, and my front tooth throbbed.

It wasn't the first time I endured a minor head injury after playing the fool and putting myself in the way of danger disguised as good fun. When I was about eleven, a concussion sent me to the emergency room. The Flourman family was visiting from southern Minnesota, where we had lived for four years. The Flourmans' middle child was a boy, Brian, about thirteen. Kay and I were horsing around with Brian and his younger sister in the basement, with its red shag-covered concrete floor. Brian asked me if I wanted to do a flip, and I naively said, "Sure!" He instructed me to bend over and stick my hands between my legs. He crouched behind me and grasped my hands. That was the last thing I remembered. He yanked hard, pulling my hands between my legs with the intent of flipping me over. Instead, I conked my head on the concrete and passed out. Like a dizzy blonde, I must have asked "What day is it?" and "What time is it?" a hundred times after I came to, my parents said. I had no memory of it except putting my hands through my legs at Brian's direction.

Curt felt as sorry after kicking me as Brian Flourman did after flipping me, but the consequences of the unintended kick lasted longer.

Three days went by, and that tooth started turning colors. It definitely was grayer than the rest of my teeth. A visit to the dentist was in order. My childhood dentist Dr. Shippingheimer determined the tooth was dead, and he performed an immediate root canal. If I had had as much time to ponder the torture of a root canal as I did the pain of piercing my ears, I never would have had the gumption to show up at Dr. Shippingheimer's office.

The tooth at the front of my wide toothy grin was a barely noticeable gray because blood had seeped into it in the days between the injury and the root canal, and it would remain discolored and slightly out of alignment, marring my goofy smile for two decades before a new dentist with new technology would put a crown on it.

+ + +

At swimming lessons, I finally started gaining strength. I didn't get as tired and waterlogged in the pool. And I got my period on a Thursday so it was done by Tuesday. I didn't have to worry after all. Relief washed over me like so much chlorinated water.

One of the ladies who took swimming lessons with us struck up a bawdy conversation with Amy and me after lessons. The lady was what at the time seemed significantly older—21 and married.

"Do you girls know self-defense?"

"No," I said as I self-consciously toweled off.

"You should, you know," she said. "I do, and I beat up two guys once. They attacked me in a dark alley."

"Wow," Amy and I said together.

"I could show you," the lady said. And she proceeded to show us some techniques that might have been karate or judo or some other wax-on, wax-off moves.

After her mini lesson, I figured I could scratch, kick, chop, punch, pound, grind, flip or turn *anyone* who was attacking me, a rapist or just someone who wanted to beat up on me. The perception of power flooded me with enthusiasm, and I was still keyed up two hours later, lying in bed and supposed to be falling asleep. I wasn't even tired. So I pondered how I would resolve Gwendolyn's dilemma with the clarinet-banjo duet that Jill had tossed my way.

Craig asked me to the movies. I didn't want to go, especially after he scared me on Amy's porch, but the polite Minnesota-Nice-Girl in me couldn't conjure up a plausible excuse, so I agreed. Then he passed me a note in science class that said, "Do you mind if we hold hands and neck?"

"That's what he *said!*" I was aghast when I told Jill in the hall after class. I shoved the note into her hands and she received it like it was used toilet paper.

"Calm down," she said, handing the note back to me. "Just ignore it until he asks again."

"What about the movies?"

"Go. Just pretend you forgot about the note."

So on Easter weekend, Craig and I went to "On Golden Pond" together. Fortunately, he didn't offer to take me on the back of his bike; we walked. Craig managed to cajole one of his dorky friends and his friend's twelve-year-old cousin to tag along, and I got Cindy, Valerie, Tonya Palomino and another girl to attend for moral support and an excuse to avoid whatever necking Craig had in mind.[32] Bringing Tonya was a gigantic mistake though. She sat behind us and giggled through all the sad parts of the movie.

Mom and Dad knew nothing about me going to a movie with a boy; I was strictly forbidden from dating until I was sixteen but I reasoned a lie of omission was not a lie at all. And besides, the entourage prevented whatever the event was from being classified as a

---

[32] Craig might have been my first real kiss but he sure as heck wasn't going to be my first real date!

date. I didn't even like Craig! He walked me home, and there were no reminders of his request and no repeat performances of the dare. I summed up the date (or whatever it was) in my diary in one word: "Yuck."

Despite his efforts, Craig got little of my attention. I was excited about the school dance scheduled the weekend after Easter.

All my hopes and plans dissolved, however, when I found out Mom and Dad were scheduled to be chaperones. I firmly believed my parents yelled at me more than anyone else's parents yelled at them. There would be no walking around town and making grand entrances. At least Amy bailed me out by inviting me to sleep over at her house, so we wore matching football jerseys to the dance.

Brent-the-Cheese was there this time, and I kept hoping he'd ask me to dance even though it felt like Mom and Dad were watching my every move. As it turned out, it didn't matter. Brent danced with everyone *but* me—even a slow one with Krista, my co-editor on the yearbook. *Gag me with a spoon!* I danced two slow dances with members of the Future Farmers of America and one fast dance with Craig's dorky friend from the movies which I suppose drove Craig mad.

Part of the evening, I stood in the seventh-grade corner of the dance with Kay and her girlfriends.

Kay pointed out one of the taller boys in her grade. "He's got big balls," she said.

You're weird, I thought.

After that, I hung out with Amy and my friends.

Kay found it amusing to embarrass me, so she walked up to Todd-the-God and told him I liked him. "Stick it," he said, she told me when she gave me the full report. I responded by punching her arm. (Diary entry later that night: *What a pest! I hate her!*)

Spring was legitimately in the air, and it finally was becoming temperate enough, even at night, to walk several blocks at a time without getting frostbite. Since I was sleeping at Amy's, I didn't have to abide by my parents' ridiculous curfew, so Amy and I walked to the Pizza Dena after the dance. Craig and his dorky friend followed us there, so we ditched our French fries and walked to the bowling alley where the most interesting male in the place was a big mouth who devoured all our hard-earned quarters: Pac-Man. Amy and I, ever the competitive friends, played video games for an hour before going home.

+ + +

The yearbook Krista and I had been working on all year finally arrived. Though we had a cast of thousands working on the project, including Amy, Scott Briller and Craig, there were some embarrassing mistakes.

"The yearbooks arrived yesterday," I told Amy, Jill and Cindy Saturday evening when we were sitting around my house, bored and looking for something to do.

"Great," Amy said. "When do we get to have them for people to sign?"

"Not until May 10th or 11th," I said. "We have to have a ceremony."

"Cool," Cindy said. "Will you guys sign my yearbook?"

"Yeah," I said, taking a nervous bite of a cream-cheese-filled chocolate cupcake my mom made for us and ignoring Cindy's concern about getting signatures. "They're kind of gross."

"What do you mean, 'gross,'?" Jill said.

"Well, all the pictures on the cover are gray, but the words I hand-lettered are black," I said.

"So?" Amy said. "Please pass the milk."

"Well, I don't know why the pictures aren't dark enough. And whoever did the cheerleaders page cut off all their hands," I said, handing the carton across the kitchen table.

"Better than cutting off their heads," Jill said.

"And on the page with the pictures of the band twirlers and the special ed kids, the headline says 'Special Olympics Twirlers,' like Tonya Palomino twirls for the mentally handicapped kids," I said, emphasizing "mentally handicapped." Amy's older brother had Down's Syndrome, and she didn't like the word "retarded" so I was trying to be respectful.[33] Amy didn't notice; she was more interested in the cupcakes on the plate in front of us.

"Oh, that's rich," Jill said smirking.

"And the headline is right next to a picture of Carrie Williams in her band majorette uniform," I said, trying to hide my smile.

"That's perfect," Jill said.

"And the pictures of the FFA and the stamp club are so out of focus, you can't even see who's in the picture," I said.

"Who cares who's in stamp club," Jill said.

"*I'm* in stamp club!" I was indignant.

"Did anyone look at this before it was printed?" Amy said incredulously, carefully picking a cupcake paper off her confection and inspecting it. "Aren't *you* editor?"

"Yeah, I'm editor, but I've never done this before," I said, feeling the hair the on back of my neck rising.

"Who cares," Jill said dismissing all the mistakes with a wave of her hand. "Nothing's perfect."

---

[33] Or what might now be called "politically correct." Or possibly just "kind."

"Craig did a cool page with a bunch of pictures in the shape of an Indian head,"[34] I said. "You're on that page, and so are you," I said, pointing at Amy and Cindy, "and so is my dumb sister with her mouth open, mugging for the camera."

"Hey, I'm not dumb!" Kay wailed from the living room where she was apparently eavesdropping on our conversation.

"Well, you can't fix the mistakes now," Amy said. "I just can't wait to have it so I can start getting people to sign it."

"And *I* can't wait until Tonya Palomino sees she's a 'Special Olympics Twirler,'" Jill said.

CINDY, ME, JILL AND AMY DEVOURING CUPCAKES LIKE WE WERE TEENAGE FEMALE VERSIONS OF COOKIE MONSTER

Our conversation deteriorated when we decided to embark on a cupcake-eating contest. The cupcakes cooling in the muffin tin in the center of the table were just too enticing.

---

[34] Wadena's mascot was an Indian before Indians were re-termed American Indians or Native Americans or indigenous people. Or whatever was considered politically correct at the time.

We stuffed cupcakes into our mouths as fast as we could while Dad took pictures. When Cindy, the skinniest of the four of us, won the contest by consuming seven cupcakes, we laughed until we cried.

"I can't believe you ate seven cupcakes!" I wailed, wiping tears from my eyes.

"I can't either," said Cindy, leaning back in the kitchen chair looking supremely satisfied. "Who's going to carry me home?"

+ + +

The month that began with a kick in the mouth ended with one, too. Shortly before we officially distributed the yearbook, Indian Tracks 1982, Valerie pulled me aside and whispered a terrible announcement.

"I'm moving away," she said.

"What? When? Why?" I blathered, louder than I had intended.

"My mom got a job in Brainerd and we have to move," she said. "All my stuff is packed in boxes, and tomorrow is my last day of school here."

Brainerd was only forty miles away, but for a girl who couldn't drive, it might as well have been Mars.

"How can you move before the end of the school year?" I asked.

"I don't know. My mom is dumb. I don't have a choice."

Valerie wasn't in my immediate circle of best friends, but we were close. I was heartbroken but not as sad as Valerie who obviously was used to saying goodbyes. My close friends—Amy, Jill and Cindy—had lived in Wadena their entire lives. I was the odd man out in that respect, having moved to Wadena in fourth grade. So Valerie, who moved to Wadena less than two years before and was moving *again*, was a strange gypsy in our small town.

"I'll write you letters," I said, trying to make her feel better. "Hey, and maybe I can get my yearbook early so you can sign it."

"Sure," Valerie said, the yearbook being the least of her worries.

Because I was an editor, I talked Mrs. Cumberland into letting me secret away a copy for Valerie to sign. Under a picture of her sinewy self wearing a bandana in basketball practice, she scrawled "Tubby" with an arrow pointing to her stomach, and she wrote:

> Moni,
> The only one I could really tell anything to. I love you. And you're special. Never change or *I'll* hold you down on the couch and kiss you!
> Love, Valerie
> P.S. We'll see each other a lot. I promise.

As usual, Valerie was bold, this time with her feelings and a joke about the Truth-or-Dare party.

May 7, 1982

Dear Diary,

Well, I kept up the practice of writing in my diary every day for April. But now I quit.

12

JILL HANDED ME *A Novel Idea* before first period. She left me with another horrifying cliffhanger with Gwendolyn being propositioned by her teacher, and I didn't know how to resolve it. I set the pages for *A Novel Idea* on the top shelf of my locker next to the Bonnie Belle lip gloss, where they wouldn't get lost, and slammed my locker shut.

Now began the rush to the end of the school year. "May Day—one of Gwendolyn's favorite holidays," I thought ruefully of my imaginary character who seemed to be dumped by a guy every holiday. It seemed like everyone was pairing off, and it seemed equally clear that Brent-the-Cheese was toying with me. Instead of boys, I focused on a different obsession: Money.

At fifteen, I qualified for driver's training and a learner's permit. Driving was the teenage equivalent of freedom and even though I had no interest in cars or horsepower, I liked the idea that I would be able to drive myself places when I turned sixteen. I attended a meeting about the driver's training program and behind-the-wheel training. "It costs $85," I wrote in my diary. "Wow. I'm glad I don't have to pay."

Eighty-five dollars was the equivalent of forty-two to eighty-five hours of babysitting, depending on the client and my method of accounting. Babysitting was my main source of income, and I had already lined up a summer gig watching my mom's hairdresser's twin seven-year-old boys, who would turn out to be a real handful for a measly $1 an hour. With an attitude of "anything's better than nothing," I agreed to the terms. I would learn to hate Tommy Tutone's song, "867-5309." The twins were obsessed with it and replayed the vinyl single on the tabletop stereo until I considered the consequences of child abuse. I got what I deserved, though, when they locked me out of the house—exactly what I once did to one of my babysitters from across the street.

When school was in session, I was babysitting up to four times a week, sometimes twice on Saturdays. The Haskels, with an obnoxious four-year-old boy and a baby, were heavy users of my services. "I'll bet that kid with the big mouth tells his parents something mean about me," I wrote one Friday night. I babysat there again Sunday and Wednesday, so either the kid kept his mouth shut, or his parents considered the source.

One Sunday afternoon at the Haskels, I went for a stroll with the kids and figured out where Brent-the-Cheese lived. His neighborhood was a new development on the edge of town, impossible to walk to unless I was babysitting the Haskels, so Amy and I never had the opportunity to casually case the joint.

Do you suppose Brent likes me and would go with me if I only gave him the chance? I mused. *Maybe I should give him that chance.*

Brent was always coming into classrooms where I was between classes, like he had memorized my schedule. He always had some excuse to talk to some other boy in the room.

I wondered if his behavior was coincidence or planned, but I didn't get to find out. Tonya Palomino started wearing Brent's letter jacket. Besides looking out of place in the spring weather, she looked like she was drowning in it. It was just like Brent to go for a flirt. I wished I could flirt and have more friends. At the last dance of the school year, Ike O'Trell asked me to dance, and then I asked him. Brent ignored me all night but he had the gall to ask my sister to dance—a slow one no less! He was just baiting me, but I wasn't bright enough at the time to realize it. I acted like a fool and asked a seventh grader to dance; then he asked me to slow dance, which wasn't much of a revenge given how short those seventh-grade boys were.

So much for my Fourth Quarter Popularity Plan. My class of 131 voted for next year's class officers, and my name was so far down on the ballot, it was invisible. Liz Sullivan, who played drums with me in band, earned the right to be called Mrs. President; popular Ana Arrowman, who put the "party" in "political party," was a heartbeat away with the title of vice president. I would have settled for vice president, I thought. My yearbook co-editor, Krista, won treasurer. I didn't even get enough votes to be voted to student council where the real work of student life was performed.

I was disappointed in myself, and I felt like my social life was the pits. "I can't act shy and I can't flirt. No one will ever like me," I lamented in the pages of my diary.

+ + +

"And I want to thank Mrs. Cumberland for being such a great advisor and trusting Krista and me with such an important project," I said, and the whole auditorium erupted in applause.

I stood at the microphone on stage after my ponderous speech, nodding and absorbing the attention of the entire junior high assembled for the yearbook dedication ceremony. I had dressed carefully for the occasion: white ruffled shirt, a bright red skirt Mom had made me for Easter, and my blue shoes. If red, white and blue worked for America, it could work for me. Krista stood next to me, and the yearbook staff sat on folding chairs behind me. Everyone was applauding, even Brent-the-Cheese in the fourth row.

Brent had just been the recipient of a Gotcha award, one of a few construction paper titles bestowed on deserving ninth graders by the yearbook staff. We named his "The Pucker Up Award" because we had a candid shot of Brent puckering up for the camera on one of the pages in the yearbook but I liked the double entendre. Amy got to present it, lucky girl. I got the "Class Brain Award," a drawing of a wormy brain adorning my construction paper certificate.

Maybe the other kids were just glad to get out of class, or maybe they wanted to get to the part where they'd get their yearbooks so they could page through them looking for pictures of themselves, but I felt important and enjoyed the moment. If I couldn't get attention from the opposite sex or earn popularity currency, I would relish the attention for my work.

After the ceremony, the accolades continued.

"You've been an exceptional editor," Mrs. Cumberland said. "We'll miss you working on the yearbook." I sparkled like a firecracker in my red-white-and-blue ensemble.

"You're a great editor!" said the girl who did the Special Olympics Twirlers page.

"It was a fun year working on the yearbook together. We got to be great friends," Bonnie told me. Bonnie was the girl who extracted the information about Brent liking me (or not) from Valerie.

"Congratulations on a great yearbook!" Mr. O said.

"You did a great job on the yearbook this year," said one of Craig's Dungeons and Dragons buddies. "I would have cracked under the pressure."

"Well, it's been great becoming friends together," Krista said. "And fun being co-editors together. You've changed since I first met you. You've become prettier and skinnier and so sweet."

Wow! She called me sweet!

I hoped that I would get a whole lot of signatures in my yearbook since I was editor. *I should get more than last year at any rate,* I thought. In the end, seventy-one friends and teachers signed my yearbook, the single greatest accomplishment of my junior high career.

My favorite teachers wrote the sort of things that would stand the test of time.

> Thanks, Monica, for making our drafting class more enjoyable." ~ Mr. Rockman

> You have a fine and curious mind without being obnoxious or superior. I admire you for this. ~ Good luck, Mr. O

> Monique, I am happy to have the opportunity to tell you how impressed I have been with your decorum and knowledge this year. Thank you for all your help in class when no one else was as curious. Your future is bright! Choose your college and man

carefully because you deserve the best! ~ Mr. Murphy

Only Mr. Murphy called me "Monique," and it made me feel special even if it didn't mean anything. Likewise, a number of the student signatures were pure flattery, like this one from Tonya Palomino who had taken to wearing Brent's letter jacket:

> I don't know what to write to someone who's tall, pretty, smart and that I'm highly jealous of, but I hope you had a great year. Have fun this summer, take care and always stay just the way you are!

Or this one from Carrie Williams, the basketball hotshot with the goddess-like hair:

> To the smartest girl in ninth grade,
> You're a real nice, sweet, intelligent person and I love your hair! I hope next year you and I can be in my dad's history class (just for fun) together and many more classes! ~ To my good, good friend, love, Carrie

Whatever she wrote in my sister's yearbook was "a lot nicer—better," according to my diary. Because of my seventh-grade sister, I got several wishes for an enjoyable summer from her friends, and Kay wrote this:

> Hello Monica,
>
> This is your beat-up machine! Thanks for being there for me to talk to you and thanks for telling me your secrets! ~ Friends always and sisters forever, Kay

Boys signing my yearbook thrilled me, even the boys from the Future Farmers of America. But some sentiments were perplexing, like Scott Briller's grammatically incorrect scrawl on the page of the wrestling team, a group I had nothing to do with:

> You was a good wrestler, Monica. ~ Scott

After much build up and endless empty promises in the last days of ninth grade, Brent finally signed my yearbook.

> Monica,
>
> I know I've been annoying you, but I don't know why. You're not really that bad. I have to admit I danced with Kay just to make you mad. I'm sorry. Well, I hope to see you around even though you probably don't think so, so goodbye and hope to see you next year. ~ F/F[35], Brent

Brent was friendly in the most platonic way, but I had to get it through my head that he didn't like me.

---

[35] "F/F" was shorthand for time-pressed ninth graders expressing the sentiment, "Friends forever."

My close friends pulled no punches.

> Problems, problems. The world is full of problems. Good thing you've got some good solutions. ~ F/F, Confucius (Jill)
> P.S. Sorry, I'm not gay.

> You're a really, really, really good friend. Even when you're obnoxious. ~ XO Love, Me [Amy]

> You are a good friend and we had a pretty good year, except for the fact that our friend Valerie moved, right? Maybe this summer we can do something fun like stuff homemade cupcakes down our mouths, right? But I'll probably be too busy becoming a famous author (Gwendolyn Joy Hayes, etc.) and you, a famous something else! Well, pumpkin head, I guess I've taken up enough room now and if Craig D. does anymore gay things, let me know, OK? ~ F/A[36], Cindy

+ + +

As the weeks of swimming lessons wore on, I fretted about the final test.

Joe, the instructor, was a fire plug of a man, about 5 feet tall and muscled like a football player. He had a military attitude about his instruction, scaring me into believing I would never pass if I couldn't prove I could save the bulkiest, scariest, poorest swimmer in the

---

[36] A variation on F/F meaning "Friends Always." See what I meant about Cindy being just a little bit different?

state. The final test required candidates to save *him*. He would jump into the deep end of the pool and resist all efforts to be saved the way a panicked swimmer might in a real situation.

I was terrified.

First of all, to save him, I had to throw my skinny arm around his chest—his naked chest—as he flailed around in the water. And then, while he continued to squirm within my one-armed bear hug, I had to swim twenty-five yards to the edge of the pool.

All the confidence the lady with the judo moves had instilled in me weeks before evaporated as I watched other students in the class bob up and down in the water fighting with the faux-panic-stricken Joe. He was as talented an actor as he was weight lifter.

Amy went first, and I silently cheered for her while taking mental notes. By the time she reached the edge of the pool with Joe in tow, she was out of breath and her hair askew. But she made it. I didn't care what I looked like either. I just wanted to survive.

My saving Joe lasted no more than ninety seconds, but I felt like I was in the water wrestling with him for an hour. I swallowed enough water to embarrass myself in front of all the other candidates, but I made it. I saved Joe. I was officially life guard material. What an accomplishment! I floated on satisfaction and joy, reminiscent of how I felt when Mrs. Cumberland told me I was a good yearbook editor.

Above all else, I was relieved to be done with swimming lessons, but Amy was inconsolable. She had to say her last goodbyes to the assistant lifesaving instructor with no body hair.

+ + +

When the yearbooks were officially released, I passed Valerie's yearbook around to be signed. During the brief weeks before the last day of school I wrote her three letters and then I quit. Some friend I was.

I tried to cheer up Amy by suggesting a new physical challenge to replace swimming lessons: Running. Neither of us enjoyed running, but we were determined to prove to our gym teacher, Mrs. Johnson, that we didn't suck.

I disliked Mrs. Johnson because she gave me C grades in gym in seventh grade, but I had earned A and B grades in eighth and ninth grade in part because I had figured out how to look like I was trying while I was hating whatever new sport we were learning. As the tallest girls in our grade, Amy and I represented Wadena's basketball future in terms of forwards or centers, and Mrs. Johnson was the coach who would decide that future. If we could keep up with Carrie (the blonde, ball-handling wonder) on the court, maybe we could play on the varsity team next season instead of just warming the bench.

"Where should we run?" I asked Amy as I stood in her doorway wearing pink terrycloth shorts and a matching top.

"Around the block?" she shrugged.

"We've gotta go farther than that," I said. "How about the pool block?"

The municipal pool was situated on an enormous chunk of land that also housed a couple of tennis courts, at least two baseball fields and the parking lot for the outdoor hockey rink. It was roughly three-quarters of a mile around.

So we started running around the pool block a couple of times every night.

Our resolve lasted about as long as my promise to write letters to Valerie.[37]

We tried a new approach with Mrs. Johnson. The week before school got out, Amy and I helped Mrs. Johnson clean up the locker room storage closet. If we had to appeal to Mrs. Johnson's baser instincts to play her game, then helping muck out a closet was part of it. If I ever hoped to played varsity basketball, I needed to impress her.

I discovered an unclaimed jacket and one of my socks in the lost-and-found box when we sorted it out. Then we unearthed a plaque lauding Valerie's accomplishments in basketball. One day in June, her absentee dad came and picked up her yearbook and the plaque. He delivered a brief-but-sincere letter from her to me signed, "Love and other indoor sports, Valerie." It was the last letter I got, and I learned long-distance relationships were hard to maintain. But that's not the only lesson I learned from Valerie, who would soon be teaching me about the dangers of playing with fire—especially the fire burning in hot older guys.

---

[37] Decades later, when I was about to turn forty, I ran—or mostly ran—a marathon with Jill. Despite crossing the finish line mere minutes before it was disassembled, that feat remains one of my proudest moments. I ran. A marathon. And I finished.

August 14, 1982

Dear Diary,

P.S. I just remembered something important. One day during break in driver's ed, I walked over to the pool and saw Brent with David. I talked to him like he was a human being. It was nice. He even talked nice back to me.

13

I SAT DOWN AND threw the pile of papers that was *A Novel Idea* on the table of the so-called Hamster Cage. It was the last day of school, and I should have been happy.

"So, we're writing a paranormal mystery then," I said.

"Yup," Jill said, looking down and picking through her chicken chow mein.

"I think it's cool," Cindy said. Obviously, Jill had cleared the story twist about a fortune teller with Cindy but hadn't consulted me. "It's like that mystic we had for lyceum. She was eerily accurate."

Amy just nibbled her granola bar in teeny-tiny bites.

"I don't think I'm allowed to believe it," I said. "It's like the song about that hotel in California that is actually about Satan. Mystics and palm readers are black magic."

"'Hotel California' is about the devil?" Jill looked up and laughed. "That's ridiculous. My brothers listen to that album all the time."

"I think Gwendolyn needs to be older," Amy said, apparently trying to change the subject.

"I don't want to write about a witch and fortune telling," I said.

"For your information, you were the editor of the *yearbook*," Jill said. "You're not the editor of *A Novel Idea*. You're a writer. Just like the rest of us."

I looked at her, and then I rolled my eyes while eating the crumbs leftover from my granola bar. "Thanks for reminding me because I forgot," I spit out the words like they were the school's chicken chow mein. Jill was right, of course, but I didn't like that she said it.

Progress on *A Novel Idea* slowed during summer break. I hardly saw Jill because she babysat at the Haskels all day every day, and Cindy vacationed at her family's cabin in Park Rapids. Amy and I worked hard at basketball camp together for a week, but we didn't practice at all when we got back. Our counselor at camp had enormous boobs. On hot days, there were wet spots on her tank top where her nipples were, like she was nursing. It was gross. For Amy, the whole week was an unwelcome intrusion on her tanning time.

The four of us got together once, in June, to celebrate Cindy's birthday.

We ate taco salad for supper, then we played cards in my parents' pop-up camper in the back yard and ate pizza, popcorn and chips like we were death-row inmates devouring our last meals. Jill gave Cindy a bottle of Catawba; it looked fancy but it was only grape juice in a wine bottle. We drank the whole bottle and wanted more, so while Cindy and I acted nonchalant and distracted Mom and Dad by making popcorn in the house, Jill and Amy biked to the Super Valu grocery store in the rain. In an "it takes a village" moment, Amy did not evade observation; she ran a stop sign on her bicycle, and a police officer stopped her. Red creeped up her face as she made excuses to the cop; Jill just kept riding. Irony ruled the excursion because we had been talking earlier about getting stopped by the police, and Amy had been the only one who hadn't had a run-in yet.

"That was priceless!" Jill recounted to Cindy and me when she and Amy got back with the ill-gotten Catawba.

"No it wasn't," Amy pouted.

"He kept calling her 'Sonya' because she had her sister's jersey on," Jill laughed.

"I can't believe he stopped me on my bike," Amy said.

"I can't believe that either," I said. "The cops are always watching."

Drunk on the sugar from the Catawba and radioactive orange stuff coating the Doritos, slumber party talk eventually strayed to boys and kissing.

"I wonder if Craig is lurking around outside," Jill said.

"He better not be or he'll be in trouble," I said.

"I wish the assistant swimming instructor was lurking around," Amy said. "I would totally kiss him."

"I wonder what kissing is like," Cindy said.

"Gross if it's on a dare," I said knowingly.

"My sister says French kissing is great," Amy said.

Jill made a face.

"That sounds gross, too," I said. "Who wants somebody's tongue in your mouth? Disgusting."

We fell asleep to the sound of raindrops on the canvas above the beds. I lay in bed thinking about boys and other scary things, like getting stopped by the cops and French kissing. Occasionally, my thoughts were punctuated by thunder.

+ + +

Babysitting, driver's training and a three-week family camping trip filled the rest of my summer.

Joseph and John, the irritating Tutone twins, defined the word "hellion" times two. But I earned enough in June to end up with $180 in the bank.

Driver's education classes turned out to be fun when Mr. Eastman, a short, bald man with a slight beer belly, assigned me to sit in a corner of the room populated by boys, including Mick and several boys who were one grade older than I was. I basked in the attention of the opposite sex. We joked around during class and on breaks. Maybe they'll remember and say "hi" in the halls this fall, I hoped silently. I studied the Minnesota Driver's Manual like my life depended on it,[38] but even the driving simulator was easy to master.

Our family went on a road trip to California in July. Five of us — my parents, me, my 12-year-old sister and my nearly 10-year-old brother — piled in the car and the pop-up camper. This is how I summed it up in a single diary entry: "We went to DeSmet, Black Hills, Mt. Rushmore, Yellowstone, Salt Flats, Reno, Sacramento, Golden Gate Bridge, Los Angeles, Disneyland, Phoenix, Grand Canyon, then through Nebraska, Iowa and then home. I took care of maps and the budget. It was kinda boring but enlightening."

That excursion was the trip of a lifetime. I'm sure it was the longest vacation my entrepreneurial father enjoyed to that point, and he smartly worked in every geographical and commercial highlight between Minnesota and the West Coast. My parents must have planned for months to figure out the logistics of this three-week camper trip.

---

[38] Given the gore depicted in the films broadcasting the benefits of wearing a seat belt, my life probably *did* depend on it.

And my assessment began with "boring" and ended vaguely with "enlightening."[39]

ME, TANNED, TERRY-CLOTH BECLOTHED AND TRIUMPHANT

Between awe-inspiring landscapes, I worked on solving Rubik's Cube (at Wall Drug, I found James G. Nourse's book, *The Simple Solution to Rubik's Cube*; reading that helped immensely[40]) and scratching the mosquito bites on my ankles until they were raw and bleeding. I just couldn't help myself.

---

[39] Oh, how hard it is to impress a teenage girl! If it wasn't about boys, I wasn't interested.

[40] And cemented my perception that answers to all of life's questions could be found in books.

I was treated like a child most of the time, herded around with my little sister and brother, but I felt important when Mom let me sit in the front seat and read the map. After spending a day traversing the winding roads of the Black Hills and seeing me in the back seat getting progressively quieter and greener, Mom realized I may have been susceptible to carsickness. I had longer legs than she did by then, so she volunteered to sit in the back seat with Kay and Curt. I felt powerful telling Dad authoritatively to "turn left here" or "we should take this highway instead of that one" because it looked shorter. Me! Telling Dad what to do! And he did it! I also carefully recorded all our mileage and gas purchases in a pocket-sized spiral-bound notebook. On straightaways when Dad held the steering wheel with only one hand, I peeked at the dash speedometer, wondering how I would ever control a car at sixty miles per hour. The simulator may have been easy but actually driving terrified me.

After our trip to California, I began behind-the-wheel training right away. The first day I went, I was dressed in loose Chic jeans and one of Mom's shirts; I didn't even bother to curl my hair—it was straight and held off my face with snap-clip barrettes everyone called Clippies. Mr. Pallid, the instructor, wouldn't care if I looked attractive while coming to a complete stop and looking both ways before entering an intersection.

But guess who ended up joining me in the car for training: Reeve Koroso, Mr. Perfect—described in my diary as "almost tall, beautiful hair, a super athlete, and rich."

I couldn't even drive.

Forget the everyday Chic jeans. I bought some skin-tight Gloria Vanderbilt jeans—those were more fashionable. At least in Wadena. The next day, I curled my hair and looked halfway decent but as usual around boys I found attractive, I was mute.

Mr. Pallid tried making conversation with us while we were driving but I couldn't talk and drive at the same time. Reeve could though. Listening to him from the back seat, I learned that Reeve went to France by himself and visited an old friend. That French people smell. French movies are expensive, and that he went on a bike trip while he was there. I learned that he had a cabin on Pine Lake, ate Cheerios for breakfast and had a huge boat. He mentioned he had a little brother, whom I remembered watching play basketball, and a little sister, too. And lots more, but when I recounted it later that day in my diary, I wrote "some stuff he said I don't remember and some was trivial."[41]

On Friday, I took my learner's permit driving test with Mr. Pallid. Nervous energy prevented me from eating breakfast, Cheerios or no. I passed though, with an 81. Reeve got a 92 or 94 (wow, he could even drive!). He said he was taking his real license test at the county courthouse the following week, and I wondered how he would do.

Besides seeing Brent one time at the pool, I didn't see him all summer. I didn't see Craig either, which was weird after seeing him show up around every corner during the school year. Mick and I tried to arrange a party at Hardee's, but only two of his nerdy friends and Cindy and Jill showed up. It was a disaster.

Summer was half-way decent. Nothing terrible happened. Nothing exciting happened either. But even if Craig wasn't right around the corner, excitement was.

---

[41] As if his breakfast choices weren't trivial.

October 4, 1982

Dear Diary,

Anyway, today was a pretty good day. It was kind of horrible until biology though. In biology, we are working on classification tables and my group got done right away so we were sitting there waiting until Jay asked me to come over and help his group (Darren is in his group, along with Kevin and Jon). I had fun helping them, flirting with them and everything. I just hope they don't think I'm too smart.

14

WADENA WAS A FARM town that grew up at the intersection of Highways 10 and 71, roads which barely supported two lanes of traffic, let alone four. It was, quite literally, set in the neck of the woods, straddling Minnesota's three ecoregions: a tallgrass prairie to the west and south bordered a forest of pine trees to the north mingling with a forest of summery green deciduous trees to the southeast.

Like the ecology of the town itself, the back yard of the house in the heart of Wadena where I grew up had three distinctive features: a box elder tree, a pine tree and a sprawling garden planted with neat rows of lettuce, carrots, peas and potatoes. The trees became hubs for kid activity. The knobby box elder tree was designed for climbing, and the children who lived in the house before us constructed a bench of sorts in the crotch of the tree. Eventually, the bench became a tree house, an obvious shack in the naked winter but a cozy hideaway tucked among the leaves in the green summer. For me, the towering pine tree was an irritant, its boughs intruding on the sidewalk between the house and the detached garage, but for my little brother, the sandy soil shaded by pine boughs was Nirvana. He spent entire summers excavating, building, and rerouting Tonka Truck roadways beneath that tree.

During the summer of 1982, I was not enjoying the trees or the garden. When I wasn't babysitting, learning how to drive or tripping with the 'rents, I was laying out on the back deck, an activity I attended to like I was obsessed, recording the minutes under the sun in my diary. No matter what, I intended to get a better tan than Amy. I slathered handfuls of coconutty Coppertone on my skin, longing to be "totally burnt." As I lay immobile, the bright sun passing through even my closed eyelids, I fantasized about the food I wasn't eating, counting and recounting the calories I had consumed and how many I had left for the day. After spending all summer doing Annette Capone's *Your 14-day Total Shape-Up Plan*[42] over and over again, I lost seven pounds. Calvin Klein jeans spokesteen Brooke Shields weighed 120 pounds, and she was 5-foot-10 like I was at the time, so I wanted to lose five more pounds.

Then, on to the frosting of my tanned and toned cake. All the babysitting and browsing fashion magazines paid off two weeks before school started when Mom, Kay and I went school shopping. We drove forty-five miles to Fergus Falls to shop at the mall on the prairie, the closest thing to Shopping Mecca for a girl from small-town Wadena. The parking lot alone was bigger than all of Main Street in my hometown.

I bought a pair of black corduroys, a pair of teal green wide wale cords, a striped shirt with white ruffles at the neck and cuffs, two

---

[42] Decades later I would track down Capone's book at an online used bookstore and use it for the inspiration to write a new shape-up plan for 40somethings: *How to Look Hot & Feel Amazing in Your 40s: The 21-Day Age-Defying Diet, Exercise & Everything Makeover Plan*. Rest assured, sunscreen was one of the prescribed potions.

long necklaces and two crew-neck sweaters (because I lived in Minnesota, after all, and sweaters were *de rigeur*). I also found a green Hang Ten pullover (no ruffles) and a Hang Ten catalog with a whole bunch of other clothes I wanted; I dog-earned nearly every page of that catalog. Altogether, the clothes I bought cost $130. Mom bought me two new pair of jeans, a new skirt and petticoat (which we found on our California trip), a new pair of tan shoes and the fabric for a ruffled shirt Mom planned to sew for me.

ME, SPORTING A BORROWED GUNNY SAX AND FRENCH BRAIDS

Romantic ruffles were haute couture in 1982. Every girl owned a Gunny Sax dress, typified by whimsical floral patterns, long flouncy skirts and lace.

School started at the end of August. At first it was scary at the high school, a sprawling one-story building. My classes were so far apart, I was terrified I would be late. But the high school had something ninth grade didn't: More, taller, cuter boys. All my summer efforts didn't land me an instant boyfriend which caused unending sorrow. Forget affection; my fabulous wardrobe, sleek physique and bronzed skin didn't even get *attention.*[43]

Even though my heart filled my throat when I thought about talking to him, I worked up the courage to approach Reeve in the hallway between classes.

"How did you do on the behind-the-wheel driving test?" I asked. (*What a stupid question! I am stupid!* my mind accused.)

"I got a 92," he said, giving me a megawatt smile. And then he turned back to his locker and started making out with his girlfriend with the super colossal boobs.

Interestingly, I noticed Reeve's little brother Royce had a locker not far from mine. The ninth-grade class came with us tenth graders to the high school in anticipation of the future closing of the ancient junior high school. We were the last class of ninth graders at that monolith, so we didn't have to be peons at the high school; the new ninth graders served that role. But Royce looked anything but a peon. He looked like he must have grown six inches during the summer, towering over everyone else in our row of lockers, including me. His hair, the color of Ottertail Lake beach sand was cut to feathered back from his face, reminding me of my heartthrob Shaun Cassidy on a *Teen Beat* magazine cover. Royce was as cute as his brother only much thinner. I didn't say anything to him; talking to Reeve was nerve-wracking enough. I frustrated even myself.

I also spied the president of ACT, the acronym for my church youth group that stood for Active Christian Teens; he apparently didn't realize I existed outside of church. I liked to think of him as

---

[43] Not for the first time, my hopes about the power of the superficial were dashed.

Mr. President, even though his peaceful smile and curly hair were nothing like Ronald Reagan's.

I was feeling morose until Labor Day weekend.

+ + +

Dad worked Saturday morning at the TV Center, and I worked, too—babysitting for Joe and John, the Tutone twins. They had graduated from "867-5309" to "Centerfold" by the J. Geils Band. What a hassle.

I got home at two o'clock, showered and packed for our family trip to Fairmont, about five hours south of Wadena. It was as far south as one could go and still be in Minnesota; fields of Iowa corn were visible from the city limits.

We lived in Fairmont until I was in fourth grade, and Mom and Dad still got together with their friends there occasionally. This weekend, we were visiting the family of Marv Flourman, for whom Dad once worked. The Flourmans had three kids: Scott was older than all of us, Brian who was two years older than I was, and Julie, who was my sister's age.

Brian was the stuntman who pulled my hands through my legs and gave me a concussion when I was eleven.

I was expecting the world's most boring weekend during which I would sleep and watch Kay and Julie play with Barbie dolls. And maybe, just maybe, get a chance to shop. But, at fifteen, I didn't have a choice about going. Never in a million years would my parents have left me home alone.

As I meticulously applied my lip gloss in the hall mirror, I asked Mom where Dad was.

"Well, he said he'd be home at four o'clock so I'm expecting him anytime."

"Come on, Mom, he's always late—it's 4:30 and he's still not here."

"Why don't you and Kay take the suitcases out to the car. Here are the keys."

I stuck my brush into a pocket of my overnight bag, hauled it to the car, and threw it in the trunk. I trudged back to the house to search for my new nail polish.

I found it in my sister's room.

"Kay, you fag! I told you not to use my nail polish!"

"I didn't use it!" she yelled defensively.

"Yes, you did! I found it in your room, you dummy!"

The front door swung open, and I glared at Kay as she ran into the bathroom.

"Hi, Dad," I said sweetly.

Dad let me drive part of the way to Fairmont, including a stretch along the interstate in the dark. Wadena was miles from interstate highways, and I didn't have much experience driving in the dark either, so this was exciting. And successful—not even a close call.

We arrived at the Flourmans at 10:10 p.m. Saturday night and after much hugging and offers of drinks and chairs, Kay and Julie raced upstairs with Curtis tagging along behind.

Brian and I sat in the living room listening to our parents talk. I was uneasy and felt awkward. Brian wasn't the boy I remembered—the bully who suggested stupid stunts to prove his gymnastic expertise. He was much taller than I remembered. And cuter with his wavy brown hair and long-lashed blue eyes.

He tried a couple of conversation angles.

"How's school?" he asked.

"Good. Just started."

"Teachers cool?"

"I guess so."

"Do you have a job?"

"Just babysitting. I babysat this morning."

"Cool."

Finally, at about 11:30 p.m., he got a look on his face like he just thought of a new idea.

"So, do you want to see my drums?"

"Sure," I said, thinking they were downstairs in the basement or maybe up in his bedroom.

"Cool," he said, grabbing his jacket and walking towards the front door.

"Um, where are you going?" I asked.

"To go see my drums," he said. "They're at church."

"Ooooh," I said, feeling stupid.

He turned and directed his comments at the assembled parents. "We'll be back soon."

I followed him out to his car, a light brown Malibu with a considerable amount of rust and no seatbelts in sight. He opened the door for me. "Nice shoes," he said when I got in and he slammed the door closed.

I was so glad I had worn my favorite blue satin shoes.

The church was only six blocks away, and he led me to a room behind the choir loft to show me an ostentatious tricked-out drum set with shiny ride cymbals and metal-accented drums. As a percussionist in band, I knew how to play snare drum or bass drum or crash cymbals. And I also knew enough to know I had nowhere near enough coordination to play them all at once.

He was clearly proud of his drum kit. "They cost $3,000."

"Wow," I said.

He sat down and played a few licks, and I acted appropriately impressed. Brian played drums for the praise choir at church. He looked suave and self-assured, and I felt self-conscious.

After a few minutes performing, he stood up. "Well, that was cool."

As we were walking down the winding stairway back to his car, he said, "So, what do they do for excitement in Wadena?"

"Oh, Wadena's a hick town. Everybody goes to the football and basketball games every week. No big thrill." I slid into the passenger side as he started the car. "I guess some people go cruising but I can't date until I'm sixteen so I don't."

He leaned across me to open his glove compartment and took out a pack of Marlboros. "Do they do this in Wadena?"

If I had been a cartoon, my eyes would have fallen out of my head; I quickly stuffed them back into their sockets and tried to look nonchalant "Sure, people smoke. But I don't."

He nodded and rolled down his window. "Where do you want to go?"

I naively had assumed we would be going home. "I don't know. You decide."

Fairmont was known for having five different lakes inside the city limits; it was filled with winding, picturesque streets that accommodated all the shorelines. We drove past my old house from fourth grade and on some of the back roads in that part of town. He said he was looking for a party, which were commonly held in corn fields where underage drinkers could violate the law unseen amid the still unharvested stalks. Then he took a detour out in the country because, he said, a bridge was out. Eventually, we found what looked like the party's parking lot, a bunch of randomly deposited cars in a gravelly spot off the road.

"I guess I don't want to go," he said, perhaps sensing my rising panic.

I wasn't an underage drinker, and I wasn't sure I wanted to start now, with my parents and his waiting for us to come home.

He drove back to town, and on the way back to his house, he said, "So, you can't date until you're sixteen, huh?"

I wondered briefly who had filled him in on my eligibility and then I remembered: I had.

"Yeah, I guess."

"Can you kiss?"

Thank goodness it was dark because I'm sure I turned fifty shades of pink. "No," I said slowly, thinking of my only experience thus far—a Truth, Dare, Double Dare, Promise or Repeat kiss with Craig.

"You want me to teach you?"

"Yeah, sure," I said without much certainty. *What did* that *mean?*

"I want some pop[44] first," he announced. He stopped at a gas station and inserted a couple of quarters into the lighted outdoor vending machine. "What do you want?" he called over his shoulder.

"I don't know," I said, my mind racing about what would taste best and what my mouth would taste like and what he liked. "7Up."

He got back into the car and drove to a municipal park overlooking one of Fairmont's lakes. It was deserted and appropriately dark. He turned off the car. I sat there, wondering what to do, looking at the lake.

He patted the seat between us. "Why don't you sit over here?" he said.

---

[44] A Minnesotan's preferred name for soda.

I moved over, and he put his arms around me. Heat rushed through my body in a tsunami-like wave; I felt overcome. "I don't know where to put my hands," I said.

"Put them wherever you feel inclined."[45]

He looked into my eyes and he kissed me on the lips. His face was warm, and his breath was sweet, as if he hadn't been smoking minutes earlier. Then he leaned back in, pressed his lips against mine and opened his mouth ever so slightly. I followed his lead, and then without any more preliminaries, his tongue was in my mouth, all wet and soft and warm and wonderful. I was floating in a hot tub, sweet bubbles threatening to consume me whole.

He drew back slightly. "That's called Frenching."

"I know," I said, a bit offended that he might think I didn't know what it was called just because I had no experience doing it.

We explored each other's mouths for a few minutes; I was shocked at how pleasant it felt. Then he ducked his head and began kissing my neck. He tightened his grip, too, drawing me closer. Blood rushed through me, and I felt like a glob of cookie dough must feel as it's whisked into the oven. Hot and close and bothered.

"Our parents might be wondering where we are," I said tentatively, absorbing his attention—or was it affection?—while remaining ever mindful of behaving modestly.

"I s'pose," he said as he nibbled my ear. Then he returned his attentions to my lips and he moved his hand between my legs, drawing up close.

"Oh, don't," I said, and he backed down my thigh ever so slightly.

We kissed a few minutes more, and then he whispered, "I guess you're right about getting back."

---

[45] Brian was not only a smooth talker, he was well read.

I drew away, and we reorganized my body next to his so he could keep his arm around my shoulders. His arm felt heavy and strong, and this simple act of sitting in close proximity felt oddly sexual. He started the car, backed out and made for his house.

"You kiss all right," he said as the neighborhoods whizzed by behind him.

"Thanks," I said shyly.

A few minutes passed in silence.

"I s'pose you'll be mad at me because I'm bringing my girlfriend to church tomorrow," he said.

You have a girlfriend?!

"Hey," I said coolly, "I'll be gone after this weekend. What she doesn't know can't hurt her." [46]

"I like your attitude."

When we got home, we tiptoed into the house, which was already dark. He went upstairs to his bed, and I went downstairs where his mother had shown me I would sleep. I undressed and crawled between the sheets, and fell asleep thinking about how soft and warm Brian's tongue was and how thrilling his hand felt on my thigh.

+ + +

Sunday morning, I skipped breakfast to spend a couple extra minutes on my hair, and I went with my parents to the first of two services offered at the church where Brian had shown me his drums the night before. After the service, Mom and Dad stood around the

---

[46] This book was almost titled *What She Doesn't Know Can't Hurt Her*. I wish I could reveal where this line, which sounds well-practiced, came from. Why was this subterfuge OK with me? And why did this blessing come from my aroused lips so easily? I don't know. Many, many years later, I would learn that what I didn't know could indeed hurt me.

narthex for ages, talking to all their friends they hadn't seen since their last visit to Fairmont.

When we finally got back to the Flourmans, Brian was already gone because he went to second service. So I wouldn't be able to see his girlfriend after all. *Dang! Was she pretty? Was she tall?*

Brian's mom made sloppy joes for lunch. I hated sloppy joes, so I ate only what I had to eat to be polite. I stole sidelong glances at Brian while attempting to participate in the table conversation. After lunch, Brian went upstairs to change his clothes and his mom said he had to go back to church and play a video of the morning's service on the municipal satellite TV station.

My heart fell. Bummer. I would have to play Barbie dolls with Kay and Julie.

Brian walked coolly down the steps and poked his head into the living room. "Want to go with me to the station to babysit the videotape?" Brian asked.

"Sure," I said, practically running to his car.

Instead of the church, Brian drove to "the station." The satellite station was a beat-up one-story building a couple blocks off Main Street. Inside, equipment was piled everywhere, and dust covered all of it. Brian killed a couple of spiders before putting the tape in the player, explaining what he was doing as he did it. Someone knocked on the door, and his girlfriend, Marie, walked in.

I sat up straighter and tried to act nonchalant, even though all she'd walked in on was a conversation.

Marie had short brown hair, and she was wearing a sloppy sweatshirt. She was significantly shorter than I was, and pudgy. We made conversation for about a half hour, and it was awkward. She looked at me as though I was the little girl Brian was babysitting, but she seemed uncomfortable, too. Her friendly words didn't match her tone. I learned she was a year older than Brian, and she was going away to college to study to be a nurse. Nursing was a noble profession but, overall, I thought Brian could do better than Marie.

Eventually, Marie left, and the videotape finished its cycle. We left, and Brian drove back to the church. We made our way back to his drum room. He pulled out Johnny Cougar's "American Fool" tape with songs like "Hurts So Good" and "Jack and Diane." I thought Cougar was too hard-edged and it wouldn't have been *my* first choice, but Brian liked it, so I went with it. With the music blaring, he sat behind his drum set and played along. I listened and perused his other musical selections.

After a while, he stopped. "I need a rest."

He pulled his chair next to mine and without hesitation, he kissed me. His proximity took my breath away. Mostly, I closed my eyes because it was too intense to look into his, but sometimes, when I opened my eyes, I saw him looking at me hungrily. I moved to sitting on his lap, and then we lay on top of a narrow folding table. He held me close so I wouldn't fall off. Then he lay on top of me. And then we switched so I was laying on him, my legs entangled in his. With the exception of Scott Briller mounting me for fifteen seconds during the *From Here to Eternity* kiss at Carrie's party in eighth grade, I had never been this close to a boy's body.

At one point, he put his hand between my legs and caressed me.

My jeans felt inordinately tight. "Don't ... don't do that," I said nervously.

"Why?" he said as he kissed me. "It feels good doesn't it?"

"Just because it feels good doesn't make it right," responded the wholesome little girl inside of me.

"It doesn't make it wrong either," he breathed.

"Yeah," I said kissing him hard. "Please don't anyway."

He stopped touching me like that and breathed in my ear, which sent a delightful thrill through me. He unbuttoned my shirt and unhooked my bra. Then he slid his hands down my pants. "You have good hipbones." Later he said, "I like your tush."

I didn't know where to put my hands, so I caressed his back and played with his hair.

"Can I give you a hickey?" he whispered, kissing my neck.

My eyes grew wide as I looked at the wall. A hickey? I didn't know how to French kiss yesterday, and now I was getting a hickey.

"Everyone would see it," I said, wiggling for a smidgen of space between us.

"OK, I'll give you a hickey here," he said, touching my bare breast. I breathed deeply, lost in his touch. "OK," I mumbled.

He gave me a hickey on my breast *and* next to my belly button. His wet sucking mouth on my skin was intensely pleasurable, but sometimes it hurt, too. I gazed at the ceiling, taking it all in, feeling unfamiliar waves of desire.

The music stopped, and he got up to change the tape. While he was up, I hooked my bra. He sat down with his legs on the table, and his back to the filing cabinet. I sat between his legs, my back against him as he alternately kissed my neck and touched me over my clothes.

I was trying to concentrate and figure out something to do with my hands other than rub his legs when we heard a loud rap-a-tap-tap on the door. I froze, then I jumped up, expecting Marie to enter the room, but the door was locked; Brian had planned ahead. I slipped my shirt on and buttoned it as quickly as I could. Brian unlocked the door, and his friend, Bob, came in, like all he'd interrupted was a set session. Brian and Bob talked about subjects I had no interest in. I just sat there, acting like I was listening, but I actually was thinking about how my hair must be out of place and how hot I was and how tight my clothes felt. I longed to look at the hickey on my breast, but it was a secret known only to Brian.

When Bob left, so did we, and when we got back to his house, we played video games.

For dinner, Brian and his family went to a fish fry, and our family went to the Country Kitchen. I ate almost nothing. When we got back, we all sat together in the living room (Curt was on the floor playing with some of Brian's old toys). Dad mentioned I had figured out Rubik's Cube on our trip to California.

"See if you can figure this one out," said Scott, Brian's older brother, as he handed me a confused looking cube.

I grabbed it and sorted out the colored sides in less than three minutes. "Ta da." Everyone was awed.

"How did you do that?" Brian said, mildly impressed.

I tried to show him how to solve it, but he didn't get it. I think it bugged him that I could do it and he couldn't.[47]

Labor Day Monday was filled with shopping (Fairmont had a mall!), and then Brian, Scott and I went to the shooting range to watch Brian's dad and my dad shoot skeet. The sky spit drops and the air was cold, so Brian and I left early in his rusty car.

"Cold out there," Brian said when we were on the road.

"Yeah," I said, looking out the passenger window at the sad gray landscape.

"Is there a reason you're hugging the car door?" Brian asked.

I felt shame about making out with Brian, dirty almost. I cherished my hickies and I melted when Brian kissed me, but the

---

[47] Obviously, Brian preferred the teaching role.

respectable girl on my shoulder whispered in my ear that I shouldn't have let a bad boy touch me there.

I couldn't verbalize these thoughts to my kissing teacher. "No," I said, sliding closer to Brian, but not touching him. He put his arm around my shoulders but we drove straight home without detour. Maybe Brian sensed my uneasiness. Maybe he was uneasy himself.

Parents surrounded us the rest of the day. Once, his hand purposely brushed my ass, but that was all. Soon enough, it was time to leave.

"Bye bye, Brian," I said as everyone else was saying goodbyes and making for the door. I smiled, but I made no moves to hug him. I didn't want to draw attention to us.

Though our goodbye was awkward, learning to French kiss was the best part of September, according to the careful notes in my diary. Brian was amiable and such a master of kissing, a charming answer to my princess dreams. It gave me the chills to think of how he touched me. But I shuddered sometimes, too, thinking of all the stupid things I'd said or done.

Two days later, in a search of closure, I wrote Brian a letter. Actually, I wrote it out three times, looking for just the right tone and words that conveyed my appreciation without crossing a line into some sort of weird obsession:

> Brian,
>
> I thought my send-off deserved more than a "bye bye, Brian," and a half-hearted smile so I thought I'd send you a quick note.
>
> On the way home, my mother said, "Brian is shy, I think." Ha, ha! And "He likes to work with his hands." That, I can agree with. I couldn't have

had a better teacher. Labor Day weekend '82 will always have a special place in my heart. Maybe I'm a sentimental freak, but that's the breaks.

I hope your last year in high school is a good one. If you're ever around Wadena, give me call and I'll show you around this hick town.

Monica

P.S. The hickey by my belly button is all but gone …

P.P.S. Every time I hear "Jack and Diane," I'll think of you.

Brian flipped a switch in me. Kissing him erased all thoughts of how gross it was to kiss Craig in front of that eighth-grade crowd at Valerie's party. His touch lit my sexual fire, and whenever I looked at a guy, I tried to decide if they would be a proficient kisser. No one measured up to Brian except one guy in eleventh grade with beautiful pink lips and silky hair who never would have taken the time to size me up. So I refocused on Brent-the-Cheese, though I suspected he had a twisted mind about sex. Still, I had never paid him the two kisses I owed him for making fourteen points in a basketball game a year and a half ago. I thought I might be able to interest him in repayment at some point.

Brian never returned the letter.

October 31, 1982

Dear Diary,

I went to a Halloween party with the ACT at Black's Grove. We played flashlight tag. And I kept screamin'. STUPID! I made a complete jerk of myself in front of Dean, Mr. President and Don. I brought Amy—Gary was there. Amy had a good time. I'm so stupid! How could I act so DUMB!

Tonight was the worst of October. I made a TOTAL FOOL of myself. TOTAL! Everybody likes Amy, and no one likes me…

15

JILL REACTED WITH spellbound horror to my confession of making out with a guy I hardly knew. She wanted to know everything, which I shared while we walked around the high school's main hub before first period. But then she said, "Wow. I can't believe you did that. Does he like you?"

"No," I shrugged. "He has a girlfriend."

"Why was he kissing you then?"

"I don't know. Because he likes to kiss, I guess."

"What about you?"

"I like to kiss, too."

"Right." She didn't sound convinced.

Amy was more understanding. Maybe because she was also interested in learning how to French kiss. Not one, but two seniors were paying attention to her like she was Farrah Fawcett in a swimming suit: Tall and thin John Marigold lived a half a block away from her, and dark and handsome Gary Boot went to my church. They both asked her to dance at the Homecoming soirée, my first official high school dance.

High school dances were held in the cafeteria, a sprawling, windowless room in the center of the one-story building. I stood with Cindy and Jill on the fringe, close enough to the lighted hallway windows that I could see what was going on, but not so close that people could see me clearly. I felt like someone had stuck his fist down my throat and squeezed my heart as I watched Tonya Palomino in her tight, name-brand jeans lure Brent onto the dance floor, and as Amy was led out there by another guy. Amy looked buoyant in her angora sweater and ballerina flats. I was sad and jealous and angry and ugly all at once, but I just stood there, trying to act cool.

In what was likely a record high for any dance I had attended so far, I danced four times: Once with the Future Farmer of America, once with a ninth grader, once with Mr. President (I guess he noticed me after all) and once with Brent-the-Cheese. I asked Brent to dance twice, but he only accepted the first time. About halfway through the night, I saw Craig making his way toward the knot of girls with whom I was standing. I ducked behind them grabbing Cindy's arm, snuck out a side door to go to the bathroom, and successfully avoided having him ask me to dance.

"How was the dance?" Mom asked me the next day.

"Horrible," I said.

"Why?"

"I only danced four times."

"That sounds like a lot."

"Mr. President asked me to dance, so that was the best part," I said, only I used his real name. "The other dances were stupid. And Amy danced all night. And even Jill got asked to dance by an eleventh grader. I asked Brent to dance twice, and he didn't want to dance at all. The second time, he said 'no'." Tears filled my eyes (though I fought them). "Why doesn't anyone like me?"

"Honey, boys will like you at some point. I promise you. Maybe they're intimidated by how attractive you are. Who knows. You can't rush these things."

"Why not *now?*" I said.

"In God's time," she said.

Maybe God was punishing me, I would sometimes think during dark moments before turning out the light and falling asleep. God knew I didn't really like Brian but had made out with him anyway, even after discovering he had a girlfriend. That was sinful of course. If God could work miracles, the only miracle He was working in my favor lately had to do with David Green, the boy a year older who gonged me and Valerie Stonyridge at the junior high version of "The Gong Show" two years ago. He was talking to me during band like I was a human being with a brain instead of a guileless girl he could torture. One day, he insisted we compare heights, and we stood back to back while Liz Sullivan measured us. By then I had reached the improbable height of 5-foot-10, and I was an inch taller than David. When we turned to see Liz announce who was taller and indicate the difference with her fingers, David looked strangely disappointed. I found his behavior perplexing, and I was always suspicious, wondering what mean tricks he was planning to spring on me when I let my guard down.

Amy, meanwhile, flirted with Gary Boot like he was the only guy in school. My locker was located along the hallway to the band room with all the other kids whose last names were in the second half of the alphabet—including Amy's, so her locker was across from mine. I watched as Gary stopped there between almost every period.

"I bet he asks you out before Oct. 13," I said one day.

"No way," she said, giggling.

"Way, I said. "Mark my words. I bet you a dollar."

"OK," she said like she was flirting with a boy instead of talking to me. "I hope I lose."

+ + +

The football team played Brainerd, and Mom and Dad let me ride the fan bus to see the game. It was weird sitting in the visitors' bleachers watching a football game instead of sitting with the band waiting for the next cue. Since I wasn't actually interested in the game, I scanned the crowd and I saw Valerie.

"Omigosh! It's good to see you," she said, throwing her arms around me when I walked up to her during half-time. We stood on the edge of the track as the teams warmed-up. I wore a blue sweatshirt with gold trim, and Valerie was dressed in a ruffled peasant blouse and tight jeans. A headband encircled her soft white-blonde hair, just like she always used to wear in basketball practice.

"I guess you're not a cheerleader in Brainerd?" I asked.

"Nope. I can't get a ride to practices," she shrugged. "Besides, cheerleaders are boring. Boys are more interesting." I watched her move closer to a boy who was talking to someone else. She stuck her hand in his back pocket, and he turned around. "Meet my boyfriend, Cliff."

"Hi," I said shyly.

Her boyfriend looked like he drove a pickup and would have been comfortable with a cigarette in his hand. He definitely didn't look like he was in tenth grade. He circled Valerie's waist with his arm and looked at me, sizing me up. Looking into his eyes, all I could see in them was sex. The F-word flickered through my mind. In a flash, I remembered the first time I heard that word, and I had asked my mother, "What's a fucker?" She had paused a long time before finally saying, "It's a pregnant woman." Much, much later, I looked it up in dictionary, and I realized my mother had been technically correct—the only way a woman gets pregnant is by having sex, i.e., fucking—though Mom had left out the part of the definition that said "usually considered vulgar." The way Valerie's boyfriend was touching her butt and the way his eyes caressed her chest sure seemed vulgar to me. I shuddered to think that's what I looked like when I was with Brian.

"Well, good luck," Valerie said. "Oh, wait, I have to root for Brainerd now. I'll wish you bad luck."

"You're safe," I said, as I watched her boyfriend nibble her ear. "We make enough bad luck without you having to wish it."

As I thought about the encounter, sitting on the dark bus on the way home, seeing Valerie had been awkward. I still couldn't figure her out, but she seemed even more foreign to me than before. I heard later that she was making out under the bleachers with Scott Briller. Why would she be doing that if she had a boyfriend?

+ + +

I was feeling sorry for myself the next day as I continued to brood about my lack of popularity with the opposite sex in Wadena. Because I had all the "In Search Of ..." episodes practically memorized, I agreed to crush aluminum cans for a church fundraiser to pass my afternoon boredom. Mr. President wasn't there, but Don was among the volunteers.

Don was the son of my parents' church friends. He was a senior (the same grade as Mr. President), and he only attended ACT youth group events when coerced by his parents because he usually was spending time making out with his sort-of-bitchy girlfriend. She wasn't around much now, though, because she graduated last spring and was going to college.

Fortunately, I didn't have to walk home from the can-crushing project because he offered me a ride. Unfortunately, Don was auditioning for a land-speed record with Nascar. He offered a ride to some guy who lived out in the country, too, and Don decided to drop him off first. I swear Don drove a hundred miles per hour to the guy's house and back. I was glad I had my seatbelt on. "Thanks for the ride," I said, as I jumped out of the car. "Don't drive too fast to get home."

"Yeah, right," Don said and roared out of my driveway in reverse. The wheels squealed as he tore down the street. I just shook my head.

The next night, I babysat at for the Bucholzes for the first time in more than a year. Their pink-festooned toddler was sweet. But I missed a youth group Bible study to do it. I would have called Mrs. Bucholz to cancel if I could have remembered her name. I earned five bucks. I had nothing to buy, but I did give a dollar of it to Amy. She had won the bet; dark and handsome Gary Boot hadn't asked her out. She promised me, though, that if he ever did, I'd get my dollar back.

If I had gone to youth group, I might have gotten a ride with Mr. President. Don never would have shown up to a youth group event two days in a row. I wondered if Mr. President noticed I was gone.

+ + +

Jill was the first among the four of us to turn sweet sixteen. Turning sixteen was a significant milestone. Not only would I get to drive, but I would be allowed to date, too. None of my close friends' parents were as strict as mine about the dating deadline. Amy, Jill and Cindy all had older siblings and their parents had apparently given up fighting about such things. But it didn't matter much because, at this point, none of us had landed a real, live date.

Jill's birthday was Oct. 23, and I bought her a friendship ring at Krause Drug. She invited the three of us—Amy, Cindy and me—for a supper party. If homemade cupcakes were the signature dish at my house, ripple potato chips and French onion dip were always on the menu at Jill's. Her mom made sloppy joes and birthday cake, too. I don't know what Jill wished for when she blew out the candles, but I wished she and I were closer. My confession about Brian seemed to have appalled Jill, and I felt I had more in common with Amy, who was as boy crazy as I was.

Jill's friendship ring fit as well as our relationship at that point—not very. I was disappointed, but the mis-sizing gave us an opportunity to go uptown together the next day—a Saturday—and exchange it. Jill invited Amy along. Our first stop was the photo studio, where portraits of local weddings and family Christmas photos were on display. We also paged through an album of recent senior pictures. Just about everyone in Wadena and most of the surrounding towns got their senior pictures taken at this photo studio, so that album was like looking at Wadena's version of People magazine's Sexiest Man Alive feature, which was inaugurated a few years later with Mel Gibson on the cover. Instead, I found Mr. President's senior photo. His photo looked even better than he did in person. I not-so-secretly hoped I was on his list of people to whom he'd give a signed, wallet-size copy.

Down the street, we saw a couple of guys we knew playing video games in Audio Concepts, so we stopped in. The clerk, a boy who was also a senior, knew my name and Amy's name, which we found both puzzling and flattering.

Next stop: Krause Drug to exchange the friendship ring. Jill tried on a half dozen styles from the turnaround case before settling on a ring that fit her delicate finger. I handed the clerk my receipt and the transaction was complete. In a move filled with teenage irony, after finding the right friendship ring for Jill, I ditched her to go to Amy's house. When we got there, Amy's sister greeted her with the news that Gary had called.

"Gary Boot?" Amy asked, incredulous.

"Yes, Gary Boot, you swizzle stick," her sister said.

It was looking like I was going to get my dollar back.

Amy called him, and he asked her to go with him to Nisswa, a town about an hour northeast known for a flashy indoor roller-skating rink with its wood floor, disco ball and pop music sound track. He told her Don, the reckless driver from my youth group, was going, too.

"Is this a date?" I asked when she hung up the phone.

"I don't know, but you have to help me get ready!"

Amy had only forty-five minutes to prepare for the first date of her life. We ran upstairs to her bedroom, and she started throwing outfits out of her closet so I could help her decide what to wear. She had more crew-neck sweaters than the population of Alaska, but we settled on a white button-up shirt, her best jeans and a pair of ballerina flats, because Gary wasn't all that tall.

Sitting on the edge of her bed, I watched her flit in and out of the room with an ironing board, a curling iron and bottles of perfume. I was happy for her. Not fake happy, but truly happy that the object of her intense interest had asked her out at last. I wasn't even a bit jealous, and it felt good.

I watched while she curled her hair and fretted about what to say and how to act.

"You'll be fine," I said. "He obviously already likes you."

I left a few minutes before Gary was to arrive, and as I did, Amy hugged me tight and whispered, "You're such a supportive friend."

"Call me no matter what time you get home," I instructed her as I closed the front door behind me.

Gary's timing was impeccable: Amy's parents weren't home that night, so she had no curfew. I popped popcorn and watched music videos in the kitchen at home, waiting impatiently for Amy to call.

The phone rang at 12:10 a.m. I answered it before it finished ringing the first time.

"Tell me everything," I whispered into the handset.

As it turned out, it was an honest-to-goodness double date. Don brought his girlfriend, Bitchy Beth, and drove the four of them to Nisswa. Of course, Don drove exceedingly fast. Gary paid for everything.

"Oh my God, it was fun," she said, recounting practically every skate.

"Well, I guess you owe me my dollar back," I said.

"When he dropped me off, he kissed me," she said conspiratorially.

"Did he use his tongue?" I asked.

"No! Don and his girlfriend Beth were right there in the front seat! He turned to me before I got out of the car, and he told me goodnight, and then he just kissed me on the lips."

"How was it?"

"Perfect," she said. "His moustache tickled a bit."

"Wow. Wow. Wow."

"I've got to go to bed," she said. "I have a thing for Job's Daughters tomorrow morning. Can you call me at six to make sure I got up?"

"Yes," I said, looking at the clock.

So I set my alarm clock and called her the next morning, right on time. She still sounded happy.

"Have a fun day," I said.

"I will," and she paused a second. "You're a really good friend, you know."

That made me feel virtuous. I still wasn't jealous. Just happy for Amy.

+ + +

As proud as I was of my noble cheer for Amy's good fortune, the following week made it hard to uphold.

Tall and thin John Marigold smiled at me more than once when he passed me in the hallway between classes, and I wondered if I was imagining it. I hardly knew him and we had never exchanged a word. Then I heard through the grapevine he intended to ask Amy out. I hadn't been imagining his attention, but I was getting it not because of my desirability, but because I was in Amy's entourage.

Then, one morning, as I was putting the finishing touches on my hair, John Marigold called me.

"Wanna walk to school together?" he asked.

"Yeah, sure," I said, surprised to get a call at all so early in the morning and even more astounded to find John Marigold on the other end of the line. Amy had to go to school early for something, so I would have been walking alone. "I'll meet you on the corner by your house."

I pondered what I was wearing and decided to trade my boots for my blue shoes; the blue shoes were cute, and function wasn't a priority. The day was cloudy and unseasonably cold. Just as we were getting to the high school, he asked if he could walk me to the football game that night.

"Sure," I said, daydreaming about his intentions. What if he asked me out? What would I say? My sixteenth birthday was still two months away, and I couldn't yet date. That I wasn't even interested in him, and Amy was, didn't enter my mind.

The day raced by, and I didn't get a chance to confer with Amy or Jill about John Marigold. After an early supper, I speed-walked to John's house to meet him on the corner again. But we didn't get to walk to school alone. My stupid sister and her dumb friends thought they'd have fun interrupting my walk with John with an unseasonably early snowball fight.

"Immature jerks," I said, trying to separate myself from my eighth-grade sister and her friends.

Just as we got to the band room where we would part because I had to don a drum for the pre-game show, John turned to me with a serious look. "Do you think Amy would go out with me?"

Inside, I died. How foolish I was to think John might have been interested in *me!* I tried to hide my disappointment. "I don't know," I lied. John was high on Amy's list of eligible potential boyfriends. "You should ask her." Then I hurried into the band room.

Why, all of a sudden, was my best friend the subject of intense interest to nearly every boy in eleventh and twelfth grades? All this time, I had been trying to get boys in our grade to be interested in me, and Amy pooh-poohed my efforts. Without doing anything, it seemed, her tanned and blonde self was attracting attention from all quarters. Envy burned inside of me, and I hated it.

Jill was even more jealous. When she heard John Marigold was going to ask Amy on a date, she said, "Well, if he asked me, I'd go, even if I liked someone else better."

What a know-it-all. She didn't know a thing about being asked on a date. Even I, the French kissing expert, had no experience with being the object of attention unless it was creepy attention from Craig. I suspected Jill liked Don, but she wouldn't admit it. "I don't want to waste my time on him," she said. "He's dating Beth."

Frustration mingled with envy in my heart. I didn't know where to go, what to do. No one liked me.

+ + +

Choosing a costume for Halloween was torture. Admission to the Halloween dance was only $1 if one wore a costume, so I had to come up with something that accented my figure, didn't mess up my hair and didn't require ugly makeup. Ghosts were shapeless, vampires and witches were too ugly, and "Star Wars" characters were too complicated.

I dressed as a football player.

Jill and Cindy arrived dressed in yellow and green with the words "Doublemint" and "Juicy Fruit" emblazoned vertically on their fronts. Clever, I thought, but when did they have time to collude on matching costumes?

Amy showed up in low-cut army camouflage, her waist tightly belted and her hair perfectly coiffed. Amy's costume had the intended effect of killing her audience, and she danced all night long. She danced with a drummer who was a year older, with tall, thin and oblivious John Marigold and get this: Reeve Koroso, Mr. Perfect. Reeve asked *her!*

"Everybody likes Amy, and no one likes me," I whispered to Juicy Fruit when Amy pranced after Reeve.

"You think *you're* unpopular," Cindy said.

After I danced with my friend Mick and then with his dorky friend, Scott Briller asked me to dance.

"Scott goes overboard on being eccentric," Jill said when I returned from the dance floor. "What kind of costume is that anyway?"

Scott was wearing a green Izod polo shirt and green makeup. "I think he's a preppy Frankenstein," I guessed. "Aren't those bolts in his neck?"

"He's a partier," Jill said disdainfully.

It was true, though: Scott was not only the tallest guy in our grade, he was arguably the smartest, too. Yet he was known to cavort with partiers. I caught wind of stories about kids who drank underage, and Scott was often among them. Maybe he was fighting being labeled a nerd, I thought. Obviously more effectively than I was.

Secretly, I still sort-of liked him, even though I knew he was the kind of guy who made out with Valerie under the bleachers, even when she had a boyfriend. But I had no idea how to attract his interest. We were seated together in biology class, which was fine with me as long as he wasn't wielding scissors, but whatever conversation we had always focused on the topic at hand: Biology. Not chemistry.

As at dances past, I considered asking Brent-the-Cheese to dance. When I approached his group of friends standing casually on the sidelines, he caught my eye and ran—literally ran away. Immature brat! I nonchalantly redirected to the water fountain. Scott asked me to dance twice more, and I counted my blessings that I didn't have to watch Amy from the sidelines all night. She danced with everyone but Gary. He wasn't even there.

This dance was better than some, I thought, but not much.

November 6, 1982

Dear Diary,

Kay introduced me to this new idea about friendship pins. They're small gold safety pins w/ beads on them. I made one for Jill, Cindy, Amy and Kay. Kay made one for me. Cindy lost hers—I'll make her another one. They are super neat. I guess a new girl showed them to Kay. This new girl has a sister in eleventh grade. Her name is Paige, and she's in my U.S. History class. I introduced myself to her the first day she came but I've said hardly a word since. She already made her move on a guy in twelfth grade. She's pretty and has nice clothes.

16

"WHY DO YOU ALWAYS leave me with these weird kissing cliffhangers in *A Novel Idea*?" I asked Jill while we were driving around town after school. Having turned sixteen first, she was the first to get her driver's license, and she often conned her parents into lending her the family station wagon, a gold Ford Country Squire with wood-grained body side panels and a supernaturally loud radio. It wasn't sophisticated, but it was functional.

Jill was killing time before play practice. She had landed a part in the fall play, "Where the Lilies Bloom," a story about a family of Appalachian orphans.

"I know you like a challenge," Jill said. I could see her smirking while she kept her eyes on the road and her hands at the 10-and-2 position.

"Seriously, everyone Gwendolyn *doesn't* want to kiss her, kisses her."

"Oh, the irony," Jill said. "You should be happy I didn't move Gwendolyn to Appalachia."

"I'm happy I don't have to write the word 'areolas' again," I said.

We took the long way to the theater so we could drive by the hockey rink, which was being flooded for the season in anticipation of freezing temperatures. We saw Don there, and Jill honked, but he either failed to hear us or ignored us. She just kept driving.

+ + +

My bedroom was situated at the corner of our house, steps away from the front door on the main floor. Beyond the make-shift door of hanging beads[48], my room looked like the inside of my locker, only more expansive.

The condition of my bedroom was a constant source of friction between me and my mother, who grew up in a cluttered farm house in western North Dakota and had come to find comfort in pristine surroundings in her own house in central Minnesota. Among my chores were weekly dusting and vacuuming of my bedroom, which was tricky when one couldn't see the floor.

Occasionally, I would call a truce and deep-clean my bedroom, hanging clothes in the closet or folding them in drawers, and stacking books and homework on the horizontal surfaces of my desk and dresser. But most of the time, I dropped my clothes where I took them off at night and waded through the piles to get to my bed.

K.C., the Siamese cat whose initials stood for Kitty Cat, slept with me most nights, against my mother's wishes. Like most of my transgressions in tenth grade, what she didn't know couldn't hurt her. After I crawled into bed, K.C. would join me, most often nudging beneath the covers and slumbering through the night at my feet. One

---

[48] Like in a 1960s movie about a druggie den peddling free love along with baggies of marijuana, the strings of beads in the doorway hid my piles of clothes and books, not drugs and promiscuous lovers.

night in early November, however, K.C. decided to sleep in a wad of quilts on the bed between my shoulder and the wall.

I woke at four o'clock in the morning to K.C.'s hissing. Still in a fog, I didn't know where I was, let alone why my cat would be hissing in the middle of the night.

"Shh, K.C., I'm trying to sleep."

My cat wouldn't shush. I lay there for a few seconds, distinctly sensing I wasn't alone with the cat in my room.

As my eyes became accustomed to the darkness, I saw a figure move across the opposite wall.

I sat straight up. "Who's there?!"

The figure stopped. "Don't yell, it's just me," I heard a voice say.

Terrified, I reached over and flipped on the lamp on my nightstand. Straddling my piles of clothes by the door of my bedroom stood a person wearing a knitted ski mask. Staring at me, he pulled the mask off his face.

It was Craig.

"What are you doing here?" I hissed, my heart racing.

"Returning something," Craig said.

"What? Why?" I said, still confused.

"I'm leaving now."

"You bet you are!" I said, keeping my voice low. "Get out of here now!"

I jumped out of bed in my nightgown and pushed him through the hanging beads[49] and out of my bedroom, trailing him as he made a beeline for the front door.

---

[49] Imagine the care Craig took to slip through those beads without waking me. What would I have done without my guard cat who wasn't even supposed to be sleeping in my room with me?

"I'm sorry," he said as he slipped out the door, carefully closing the screen so it wouldn't slam.

I pushed shut the main door and locked it, leaning against it and shaking my head. I couldn't believe I'd just found a masked intruder in my bedroom.

In the dark, I tiptoed to the back door and locked that one, too. Then I checked the deck door and flipped the lock on it.

Living in a small town offered a false sense of security, and we rarely remembered to lock the doors when we went to bed. Though my father had kept inventory for his television store in our garage in the past, we no longer had a reason to guard our property with compulsive care.

I tiptoed back to my bedroom and scooped up my cat.

"Thank God for you, K.C.," I said as I secured my blankets around me. As I thought about the brief encounter with Craig, I remembered he said, "I'm returning something."

I got out of bed and inspected the piles in my room. Though they looked like unorganized messes to everyone else, I knew what belonged where. Where Craig had been standing, I found a pair of my panties—only I called them underwear because panties sounded too cutesy—crumpled up in a ball and tucked under a pair of jeans. This pair of underwear was distinctive with its blue tropical floral pattern—a pair my mother bought for me when she and Dad won a trip to Hawaii the year before, for selling an impressive number of Zenith television sets at the TV Center.

I was aghast. Had Craig been returning a pair of my underwear? I raked my memory. I knew I hadn't seen that pair in weeks, maybe months. It should not have been where I found it unless Craig put it there minutes before.

But how did he get my underwear in the first place?

In the eerie silence of the night, I combed through the rest of the detritus on the floor, but I found nothing else out of place. Satisfied I'd inspected my room thoroughly, I climbed back in bed and turned out the light.

But I didn't go back to sleep. I lay there, thinking about how Craig got my underwear.

I remembered some of my other belongings that showed up in strange places: the electric blue shoe I found in my locker, the drumsticks Craig returned to my mother, the unsigned note I accused Valerie of writing.

Realization dawned on me like the sun over the horizon. Craig was behind it all. He had been in my bedroom before, maybe multiple times. He must have known my locker combination at the Junior High School, too.

I was outraged. In the strong words of a Valley Girl, how totally, totally gross! Craig was a pervert.

Finally, sleep overcame my emotions. I dreamt of shoveling the dirty clothes and old homework out of my bedroom, but I hadn't put this matter to bed yet.

+ + +

The next day, a Sunday, I fretted about what and how to tell my parents. In church, I prayed about it. "God, help me figure out what to do."

When we got home and had eaten lunch, I took a deep breath and walked into the living room where Dad was about to take his hallowed Sunday afternoon nap. He was sitting in the recliner, reading the Sunday paper. A football game played at low volume on the TV.

As soon as I started my story, he put aside the newspaper and moved the recliner to the straight-up position. Off went the television. "Karen!" he bellowed.

I told them both what happened and how I locked the doors after Craig left. I didn't tell them that I suspected Craig had been in our house in the middle of the night before.

"We won't leave the doors unlocked again, that's for sure," Dad said.

They ordered me out of the room and he and Mom huddled together to determine a course of action. I sat on my bed in my room, looking at my hands. When I was summoned back, Dad informed me he was going to call Craig.

"What's his number?" He knew I had it memorized. "Here, dial it."

I meekly followed his orders like I had been the one to do something wrong. I didn't want to stand there and listen, but I had no choice.

Dad yelled at Craig for a while. He used two swear words, but Craig deserved it. I couldn't hear how Craig responded, but I assumed Dad got his point across.

The police were never called. I spent hours on the phone telling Amy, Jill and Cindy what happened, and the game of telephone raced from there. I heard later from one of Craig's creepy friends that Craig had taken one of my bras, too. I quit speaking to Craig. Mick, who was friends with both of us, told me he felt caught in the middle.

"Don't stay mad at you-know-who too long," Mick wrote in a note he passed to me in English class later in the week.

I stuck my tongue out and crumpled up the note.

I was bummed out, too, that Craig jolted me out of our comfortable friendship. Craig's slimy actions had been laid bare like a worm on the sidewalk in a rainstorm. Craig was a worm—I didn't even like thinking about it.

In band, one of the trumpet players passed me another note. "I think you should kill Craig. That was pretty rotten what he did. C-ya." It was signed "David," none other than the first-chair flute player. The note had been passed all the way from the front row to my timpani drums in back. Nice. Everyone must have been talking about it. Craig was on the other side of the room with his trombone, eyeing me. I wanted to disappear.

John Marigold, tall and thin and oblivious, finally asked Amy out. Amy hemmed and hawed and told him she had a sleepover with Job's Daughters so "maybe some other time." By this point, John was like three-day-old cake—once sweet and appealing, now boring and verging on moldy, at least to popular Amy. I went to the Job's Daughters' sleepover as Jill's guest, but I hung around Amy most of the night. I was jealous of Amy's popularity, but I didn't want to show it the way Jill did.

"You should get Best Friend Award," Amy said.

That made me feel good, like maybe I was finally reaching my goal of being less selfish.

Gary was also so "last week" to Amy, and she decided she liked Don-the-Speed Demon. "I won't show I'm interested in him until I know he's broken up with Beth, though," she confided in me. *Hmm, I guess she and Bitchy Beth got chummy on their double date*, I thought. *And what about John Marigold?* But I was secretly happy she left him hanging after the way he used me to get information on her in the first place.

After Brent's behavior at the Halloween dance—running away! I mean, really!—and Craig's weirdo act of betrayal, I decided to refocus on Scott Briller, still the tallest, most eligible boy in our grade. I could flirt with Scott in biology, the only class we had together.

"I heard Valerie invited you to Brainerd." I was fishing.

"Yeah, but I couldn't get the car," he said.

"She invited me, too," I said. "But I can't drive."

He was performing in "Where the Lilies Bloom" with Jill, and he played a harmonica, so I teased him about playing a har*Monica*.

"Yeah, I'd like to play some more har*Monica*," he wiggled his eyebrows.

I soaked it up.

Don was in the play, too, so Amy and I had every reason to go see it. I was feeling increasingly weird about the whole Don issue, though. When Jill and I played "Tron: Solar Sailor" on my Intellivision video game system at my house earlier in the week, she was still acting like she liked Don, but her words denied it again. She wore her stubborn nature like a comfortable sweatshirt. "He's going with Beth so I don't want to waste my time with him."

Gary sat right in front of Amy and me at the play, but all he said to Amy was "Hi." He stared stonily forward after that.

When the play ended, Amy, Jill and I went trolling—Jill's driver's license was like a Freedom License; we relished driving around town with the radio on instead of just walking. We could cover more ground. Amy and Jill hoped to see Don, but neither of them admitted it, and I hoped to see Scott, but we all struck out. We also did reconnaissance on Reeve Koroso, who had given Amy a winning smile in the hallway, but he was strike three: Nowhere to be found.

I worked the ACT youth group bake sale on Saturday afternoon with Mr. President. We sat together behind a table at the Ladies Aid fall festival selling apple pies and oatmeal raisin cookies and frosted cinnamon rolls made by the moms of the kids in group. I proved capable of handling money and making change, but what I enjoyed was having Mr. President's attention all day, though I didn't have the guts to ask for a senior picture.

At one point, when our conversation about music and his obsession with collecting girls' phone numbers dwindled to silence, he asked me a hard question. "So what's the deal with Craig?"

Practically everyone in my grade knew about Craig's excursions into my bedroom, and word apparently traveled beyond my circle.

"I don't know, what did you hear?" I said.

"You tell me," Mr. President said cagily.

"He's weird," I said. "I found him wearing a ski mask in my bedroom one night."

"Just a ski mask?!" he mocked horror.

"No. Duh," I said. "A ski mask in addition to clothes."

"Weren't you scared?"

"Yeah, I guess. I don't like to think about it."

"I agree with you. He's weird."

I regretted talking about it at all. So much for flirting with Mr. President. The afternoon turned out more like a bad therapy session.

While my love life was in the sewer, my grades were impressive, at least to my parents, who believed that grades mattered, and to me, who, at that point in my academic life, believed my parents. At the end of first quarter, I got all A's, even in Phys Ed. Amy's grades were the highest in tenth grade in every class *except* Phys Ed: Mrs. Johnson gave her a B. She was mad, and I felt guilty for feeling happy about it. But she didn't have much time to pout because tall, thin, and oblivious John Marigold asked her out again, and this time, she said yes. A movie date. I was jealous of this, too, but mostly sad because I didn't have as much as a nibble in the date department.

+ + +

"What the heck are you doing to Gwendolyn?" Amy asked Jill at lunch, knowing our shared manuscript was awaiting my creative flourish.

"What now?" Cindy asked.

"Oh, Monica is upset because Gwendolyn is getting kissed more often than she is," Jill said.

"So, how was your date last night with John Marigold?" Cindy asked Amy, changing the subject.

"I'm never going out with him again," she said. "Boring, boring, boring."

I had already learned Amy didn't like him because he had sweaty palms, and he held her hand in a death grip throughout the whole movie. She told Cindy and Jill this.

Cindy sighed. "I'd take a guy with sweaty hands."

"So, how are you and Don," Amy said, fishing. We both thought Jill liked Don, but she still denied it.

"We're. Just. Friends," Jill said, emphasizing each word through gritted teeth.

"Wow, you are stubborn," I said, shaking my head. "Who's up to go to boys basketball practice with me after school?"

"Count me in," Amy said.

+ + +

Basketball season had begun again. Ah, basketball! Part of me was excited because I loved watching the boys and keeping score books for them, but part of me was sick of playing basketball. Basketball camp the summer before did nothing for my success, and, as usual, Amy and I were competing for the same spot and she was winning.

Unlike me, Brent-the-Cheese had gotten better since last season. Brent realized I was angry with him, but he said he didn't know why. I didn't think he even cared. And I didn't care either—he was frustratingly immature! I also noticed Scott Briller's legs were as hairy as Dad's. Scott and I had a laugh over molecules in biology one day, though neither Brent nor Scott were paying much attention to me. That didn't stop me from hanging around basketball practice like a groupie for Jimmy Buffett.

While we were hanging around the doorway to the gym that afternoon, Reeve Koroso flashed another one of his million dollar smiles at Amy. There was no mistaking it—he was looking at Amy—but I almost died on the fringe of the wattage. Mr. Perfect was fun to watch run up and down the court, passing the ball.

Reeve's smile helped blunt Amy's pain. Rumor had it that Gary was going on a double-date with Shelley Anson. Or maybe Tonya Palomino. In any case, it seemed apparent he wasn't going out with Amy again. Not liking Gary was one thing, but it was quite another if *he* didn't like *her*. Amy worked herself into such a tizzy telling me about it as we walked to the gymnasium, she started crying. "I thought you didn't like him?" I wanted to say, "Boo-hoo. Try being me," but I felt sorry for her, too. It seemed like Gary was a lost cause. I suspected Amy still liked Don, but now she was denying that, too.

Jill, who continued to insist she and Don were just friends, was having problems, too. Apparently, Beth came home from college the previous weekend to "babysit" Don because she heard he was dating other girls. So now Don, who was "just a friend" anyway, wasn't allowed to talk to Jill. Which was tricky, since they were both in the play together and *had* to talk to each other.

After the second-to-last performance of "Where the Lilies Bloom" on Friday night (Amy and I went to see it again), Don gave Amy a ride home (I guess it was OK for him to talk to *her*), and I rode around with Jill. Only, apparently, a whole lot happened after Jill dropped me off in time for my curfew at home.

When she was relating it on the phone the next morning, Jill sounded like a robot with the volume turned down, she was so depressed.

"So, I ran into Don last night."

"What?! You ran *into* Don's car? Or he ran into you? He's a crazy driver."

"No, not actually *ran into*. He pulled into my driveway after I pulled into my garage, so he and I drove around for a while."

"I thought Bitchy Beth said he wasn't supposed to talk to you."

"Yeah, well, he wasn't. While we were cruising, we realized we were being followed."

"By?"

"Rob Lake and Diana Green."

Diana was David Green's sister, but that wasn't the only reason not to like her. "Isn't Diana good friends with Bitchy Beth?"

"Yes. We tried to lose them. Then Don dropped me off, but he couldn't escape my circle."

Jill lived in a modern split-level on a cul-de-sac in the newer part of Wadena.

"What happened?" I was glued to the handset.

"They cornered him. Diana jumped out of Rob's car and started swearing at Don and throwing fists, like, seriously pounding on him.

Then she jumped into Rob's car, and they drove off. Don rocketed out of my circle like he was embarrassed."

"Oh, my God. What did you do?"

"Nothing. What was I supposed to do? Come to his rescue? I was already in the house, but I saw the whole thing."

"Wow."

"Yeah, wow. This totally sucks."

"Yeah, sucks."

To try to cheer her up, I bought her a pink carnation and delivered it to her house later in the day. We decided to walk around town. She couldn't have the car two nights in a row, but her parents thought she went to my house, and my parents thought I went to hers. Mom and Dad were going to a card party across town, and they said they'd be home at 12:30 or 1, so Jill and I had five hours to fool around.

First, we walked to the hockey rink, where we could escape the cold in the warming house. No one was there. So we walked uptown past the Junior High School. We intended to go to the Pizza Dena but neither of us had anything more than some spare change, so we decided to walk to the bowling alley.

We had no interest in bowling and no money anyway, so we hung around the arcade in front and played three games of Dig Dug each with our spare quarters. Avoiding falling rocks and Pooka monsters was reasonably easy, but the fire-breathing Fygar dragons got me every time. About half-way into the third game, Don showed up with Scott Briller and Paul Tanqueray, a pudgy saxophone player in Don's grade who was also in "Where the Lilies Bloom."

"Hey," Don said.

"Hey," said Jill, while she maneuvered Dig Dug to burrow around the Pookas. I leaned against the video machine and stared at Don.

"I just wanted you to know, it's all over between me and Beth."

Jill looked away from the screen and Dig Dug was burned to a crisp. "Oh."

I muscled her over so I could play my turn, half concentrating on my game and half listening to Don lamely apologize for the night before.

"It's OK," Jill said.

As abruptly as they arrived, Don, Scott and Paul left. Jill and I were stuck in the middle of the arcade talking to two girls from our grade I considered partiers. I felt like I didn't have anything in common with them, but Jill gamely made conversation for a few minutes.

"Well, we gotta go," Jill finally said, and we walked out of the bowling alley into the cold.

"Where are we going?" I asked.

"Maybe we'll see Don and Scott driving around," Jill said putting on her mittens. So we walked back the way we'd come. Conveniently, the Briller' house was on our route, and we saw Don's car parked in the street out front.

"Let's crash their party," Jill said.

"Good idea, I'm freezing," I said.

"Go knock on the door."

"I'm not going to knock on the door," I said, backing away. "You do it."

"C'mon, just do it."

"No."

"I thought you were cold."

"I thought you were a party crasher."

So we walked around the block, working up the courage to ring the Brillers' doorbell. The cold steeled our resolve, and we found ourselves on the Briller' porch, pushing the doorbell button like we were selling candy bars for the band boosters.

Scott came to the door and, causing both my heart and my freezing hands to tingle, invited us in.

As he led us to the back of the house, I realized the floor plan was more vast than it appeared from the street. The hallway was decorated with paintings in heavy frames. A rack of gleaming copper pans hung over the island in the kitchen.

In the living room, or maybe it was a den, Paul was sprawled on a leather couch, holding a glass of ice and a liquid substance. I admired the lush carpeting, and I noticed an enormous console TV; this room was a dramatic departure from what I considered the den in my house, a paneled basement room with red shag carpeting and an ancient poster on the wall from the previous resident describing how to make Harvey Wallbangers[50]. Don was sitting in a chair at the bar like a customer, and Scott took up the spot behind the bar. Jill instinctively sat in the seat next to Don. I leaned awkwardly against the end of the bar, not wanting to enter Scott's space but yearning to be close.

"Want something to drink?" asked Scott, like an attentive bartender.

---

[50] A Harvey Wallbanger, the wild cousin of a screwdriver, is a mixed drink of vodka, Galliano liqueur and orange juice. It was a marketing construction with a sandal-clad surfer mascot developed in the late 1960s to sell Galliano. It's amusing to think of the former resident of our house in the snowy land-locked state of Minnesota as a fan of a drink named for an imaginary surfer. Almost as amusing as it is to remember I was a fan of Hang Ten surfwear.

I eyed the glasses in front of Don and Scott. They looked as sinister as whatever Paul was drinking.

"No thanks."

"I'll have a diet Coke," Jill said.

Don leaned into Jill and whispered something in her ear. She smiled. He put his arm around the back of her chair.

My eyes grew round. Jackpot! I turned to Scott and made small talk, trying to ignore Don nuzzling Jill's neck. Scott pulled an ashtray from some cupboard in the bar. I watched with a mix of horror and longing as he fiddled with a lighter and lit the cigarette he held in his long fingers. He tried to read my expression, but I asked some insipid question about the music that was playing. An image of Brian brandishing a cigarette flashed through my mind; it seemed the smokers who entered my sphere were always gauging my reaction.

After a while, he announced, "I'm gonna hold Monica's hand so no one freak out."

I freaked out.

Scott's hand was warm, and I noticed he had the barest hint of hair on his knuckles. We kept talking like it was the most natural act in the world to hold hands. Paul asked some question about his drink. Don and Scott shared their opinions of different types of alcohol and their prices. I had no idea what made vodka different from tequila or how much smoother Bacardi was than Phillips, so I kept my mouth shut.

The music stopped, and Scott let go of my hand to walk across the room to change the record. I must have been holding my breath because I felt like the air had been let out of me. Sounds I would have described as punk music started playing only I couldn't name the song or the band. When he came back, he picked up my hand again.

"Cold fingers," I said, apologizing for my icy hands.

"Cold hands, warm heart," he said.

"Let's go see Wayne at the radio station," Paul said after a while. Wayne played drums with me in band; he was always friendlier to me than David Green.

"Cool," Scott said.

"I s'pose," Don said.

Everyone made moves for their coats. I watched Scott as he took the glasses, rinsed them in the sink and put them in the dishwasher.

"I get the feeling you girls don't approve of all this," Paul said.

"Whatever you guys want, just don't make me a part of it all," I said.[51]

"Well, we didn't," Paul said with a mean tone.

I felt like an ass. Why couldn't I just keep my mouth shut, I wondered silently.

We piled into Don's car, and he drove two blocks to the radio station. Jill made some excuse, and she went to Super Valu across the street while the boys went to the radio station. "We'll come up there in a minute," I said.

"Let's go home," Jill said when the boys disappeared.

"Why?"

"I'm late."

"It's only 10:30," I said.

"I want to go home."

"My mom and dad said they wouldn't be home 'til 12:30 or 1."

"I want to go home." Jill started walking away.

I stood for a second, then ran after her and fell into step.

After about a half a block, I said, "I was having fun."

---

[51] I should have been thought of as a fool rather than remove all doubt.

"Then go back," she said, walking briskly in the direction of home.

So I did go back, hoping she'd follow me. But she didn't.

When I got back to the radio station, Wayne was the only one there. He was polite, but he was working. Forget this, I thought as I walked down the stairway to the street.

Jill was blocks ahead of me on the way home, and the boys were nowhere in sight. I started after Jill, and a few blocks later, Don drove by. He was alone in the car. "Wanna ride?" he said.

I didn't actually want a ride with Don, who had been drinking and was a reckless driver in any condition, but I was cold, so I got in.

"Jill's up ahead of me somewhere," I said.

We found her about two blocks from her cul-de-sac. Don opened his window and asked her if she wanted a ride.

She ignored us. Her hands were jammed in her pockets, and she was walking with a purpose.

"What the heck?" Don said to me as his car slowly trailed Jill.

"Who knows," I said.

He parked and hopped out. "Should I wait here?" I asked.

"Sure, whatever," he said.

He walked with her, but it looked like she still wasn't talking to him. I lost sight of them when they rounded the corner, but within a minute, Don was jogging back to his car.

"Let's cruise around," he said. He turned up the radio, and we drove around for about an hour. We didn't talk about Jill or Scott or relative merits of Bacardi or anything else. He dropped me off at about quarter-to-12.

Six minutes after I went into my room, I heard Mom and Dad come in the back door.

November 30, 1982

Remembering November

Family: *My parents are getting on my back again. Every day Mom tells me to clean my room—make my bed. Yuk!*

School: *I used to think that my high school years would be the best of my life, but I'm looking forward to the end of them.*

17

I WAS BOTH ECSTATIC and confused. Ecstatic because Scott held my hand on Saturday night. Confused because he acted like he didn't know me in biology class on Monday.

I doodled in my notebook. "Scott Briller: Mr. Cool. Monica Wallgren: The square of the whole school."

Maybe he was drunk, I reasoned. He didn't like me. I was just handy. Get it? *Handy*? At least I cracked myself up.

Jill confused me, too. She told me she didn't like Don, but I found him leaning against the wall by her locker between almost every class. Apparently he had officially asked her out, then called it off because he said had to babysit his little brother. So even Jill—Jill who thought French kissing was appalling and claimed she just wanted to be friends with Don because he had a girlfriend—even Jill was dating. Or at least being asked out. What *was* it with me? Was it my charming good looks? Highly doubtful. Boys didn't make passes at girls who wore glasses. My height? Probably, but then Amy was as tall as I was. What was it then? Too smart? Unlike Rubik's Cube, my love life was a puzzle I couldn't figure out. Frustration oozed out of my every pore.

I cornered Don. "Was Scott drunk on Saturday?"

"No, not that drunk," Don said. "Just enough to wipe out his inhibitions."

+ + +

The centerpiece of Mr. Murphy's American government class every year was mock court.

Mr. Murphy was as close to a metrosexual as Wadena Senior High School would get in 1982. He wore a vest over his button-down shirt almost every day, but his signature was his facial hair. Almost all my teachers had moustaches, but Mr. Murphy's dirty blond whiskers were always well coiffed. I might even have considered him handsome except I was taller than he was. Instead, we enjoyed an appropriate mentor-mentee relationship, and he made American politics fun.

One day after the bell rang and I was making for the door, he asked to speak to me.

"Mock court starts next week, and our accused needs a capable attorney, Monique," he said using his pet name for me.

Puzzled, I said, "Your accused?"

"Sure, the guy accused of murdering Mrs. Magillacuddy in the gymnasium with a football trophy," Mr. Murphy said. "He needs a good defense."

"So," I said.

"I've assigned you and Tonya Palomino to defend him," he said.

"Do I get a choice in this?" I asked.

"Not if you care about getting an A," he said. He wiggled his eyebrows and smiled.

"Who's the accused?" I asked.

"George Gordon."

"I can't defend a guilty person," I said. No one in tenth grade, least of all me, liked George and his greasy black hair. He was weirdly confident, as if he already knew what the rest of us wouldn't learn until our first class reunion: High school popularity is fleeting.

"That's the point." Mr. Murphy said. "We don't know if he's guilty or not. That's why there's a trial."

"I can't," I said, thinking about how Tonya made out with Scott Briller last year at the Pizza Dena, how she outbid me for Brent-the-Cheese on Slave Day, how she acted so juvenile when we went to the movies, and how she supposedly double-dated with Gary, which made Amy so sad.

"If you won't be a defense attorney, Monique, I'll have to put you on the jury." Mr. Murphy said, as though he were hurt.

"I'll take it!"[52] I said and rocketed for the door, ducking out of his sight before he could argue.

+ + +

Two days later, Missy Keskikallio was absent from Mr. Murphy's government class. Not only was she MIA for the day, she was going to be gone for four to six weeks; Missy Keskikallio had a mysterious disease as long as her last name: Mononucleosis. Jill called it the kissing disease, but I didn't understand why some kissing led to disease and some didn't. Missy had been assigned to prosecute George Gordon in the mock trial, so Mr. Murphy needed a new prosecutor. Guess who got the job.

---

[52] This would be the first and last time I was happy to be called for jury duty.

Now I debated *against* Tonya Palomino. If I thought I couldn't defend a guilty person, I had no problem prosecuting someone who may be innocent. My prosecution team consisted of Carrie Williams, the basketball star with the beautiful blond hair, and Duke Christian, a burnout with an attitude.

Since I had no choice but to play a pivotal role in the mock trial, I took my work seriously and studied everything about the case against George Gordon with the greasy hair. Our case was entirely circumstantial but I was intent on winning. Losing wasn't an option.

I played the role with intensity, as I played everything else—except basketball. I hated losing, and I loved figuring out puzzles. I knew there must be a way to persuade the jury of my classmates that George Gordon had indeed killed the imaginary victim, Mrs. Magillacuddy.

The trial opened on November 14, 1982, and I wore the new red cotton sailor dress my mother sewed for me for Easter. The concept of bland navy suits hadn't yet entered the Wadena consciousness, let alone mine. I thought I looked the part of a professional lawyer but apparently good looks got me only so far. My summary of our opening arguments and presentation of the case against George was recapped thusly in my diary, "We're losing in court! I hope we get better. After all, it was only the first day."

Tonya turned out to be a creative adversary. She was as proficient at cross examining witnesses as she was at recounting her own sexual exploits.

The following day, I reported "court was better today." But our case fell to pieces on Friday, before we would take a weekend break, when a surprise witness, likely chosen by Mr. Murphy for her stubborn attitude and talent for the dramatic, took the stand.

"Jill totally screwed up everything!" I told Mom when she asked me how my day was. "She was a surprise witness—a doctor. She told the court that the janitor was drunk! He's an eyewitness!"

"Oh, dear," said my mother, the woman who spent entire weekends reading mystery novels and knew the complications such testimony would present.

"I guess we'll have to fix it on Monday in court," I said as I trudged to my bedroom to deposit my backpack and the notes from the court case.

+ + +

We played our first basketball game of the season against Melrose that Friday. We lost. I didn't make any points. Amy started. When she fouled out, Mr. O subbed in perky Christi Marans, who had grown four inches and mastered layups, at center. So I was No. 3. I hated being No. 3.

After the game, Jill, Don and I went to Amy's for pizza. By now, Amy had decided she still liked Gary, and Don was simply her friend. She was as mercurial as I was.

Dad had set my curfew at 10:30, but Don drove us around for a while after the pizza. We met the boys basketball bus when it arrived in Wadena from Aitken, and Don offered the guy from church who lived out in the country a ride home. As usual, Don drove 100 mph on the way there and back. He dropped me off at 11. Dad was sitting in the living room watching TV.

"I was worried," he said. But that was all he said as I escaped to my bedroom.

On Saturday night, Jill and Don came to my house to play Intellivision.

After we grappled with imaginary digital adversaries, Jill had her first experience with … sex (in my diary, it was noted with an exclamation point). When Don took her home, he kissed[53] her.

"How was it?" I demanded.

"I was afraid I was going to do something wrong, so I said thanks and I got out of the car."

"Oh, Jill!" I wailed. "You should have kissed him back!"

"Well, I did. I just didn't *keep* kissing him back."

"That's a bummer if you ask me."

"Do you think he thinks so?"

"Probably."

+ + +

It happened again. Only this time I wasn't jealous.

The clerk at Audio Concepts asked Amy to the Christmas dance. He was the one who knew our names when we were there the day she went out with Gary Boot. She pussy-footed around and the clerk mistook her lack of "no" for a "yes" and he assumed she was going with him to the dance. Only she wasn't. She had no interest in him. She wanted to dance with Gary and maybe even Reeve Koroso. The next day, she set things straight and broke his heart.

I never had those problems.

Meanwhile, Cindy was obsessed with Jim Whiteman. Jim was moderately tall, with wispy dark hair, and quiet, sort of the high-school-boy equivalent of his bland name. He was in eleventh grade. Cindy had about as much of a chance dating an eleventh grader as I did. Probably less—she didn't even know how to French kiss. But then Don and Jim planned a double date—a double date!—with Jill

---

[53] At this point in my education, sex and kissing were the same thing.

and Cindy. They went bowling on Saturday afternoon. I walked over to the alley and visited with them for a while. Brent-the-Cheese was there.

"Did you hear how many points Scott made at the game last night?"

Seriously? Why was Brent talking to me about Scott? "No," I said.

"Six points."

"Wow, that's cool."

Brent's eyes narrowed.

"Yeah. I scored 10 points."

"Even cooler!" I wanted to dissolve into the bowling ball gutter. Clearly, Brent knew I liked Scott. So Brent for sure must not have liked me.

"Going to the dance tonight?"

"Yeah," I said warily.

"Not me. I'm having a get-together."

"How nice for you," I said.

After being humiliated at the bowling alley, I went home to get ready for the dance. My hair refused to cooperate so I pulled part of it up and back and tied it with a bow. I used Clippies to secure the recalcitrant baby hairs in front.

I walked to the dance with Amy, and that was the most exercise I got all night. As he had warned, Brent wasn't there. Scott didn't ask me to dance. Mr. President completely ignored me, spending the whole evening hanging around with Mary Kartoffel with the curly hair the whole time. Who was Mary Kartoffel? I was appalled. Or in the parlance of the time, grossed out the door.

I noticed Craig danced repeatedly with Ivey Zwilling, a girl a year younger than we were. Craig had tried to talk to me in band, in health class, and in the hallway between classes, but I was always curt and moved along as fast as I could. Ivey was sort of weird, but she was tall. Apparently Craig liked tall. This development also grossed me out. How could Ivey like Craig? She knew what he did to me, and I thought she was thick-headed. Or desperate. Or both.

I glumly listened to the music instead of dancing to it. The deejay kept playing duds from Joan Jett and Fleetwood Mac.[54]

Jill refused to dance with Don. I couldn't figure out why, but maybe it was because Diana Green was there, watching us.

About 10 p.m., Don walked across the cafeteria and asked me if I wanted to go to a party with him.

"Without Jill?"

"Yeah, I'm only thinking about checking it out. No biggie."

I briefly weighed the pros and cons of staying at a boring dance versus stopping by a tempting party, and I figured I had nothing to lose. "OK."

He waved his arm to Scott across the room, and then there were four of us walking to Don's cold car in the parking lot: Me, Don, Scott and Liz Sullivan, the popular president of my class who played drums with me in band. Don turned the radio to a volume a few decibels louder than a jet engine and drove to Ana Arrowman's house on the edge of town. Ana, like Liz, was one of the kids who went to the Catholic school until seventh grade, so I wasn't actually friends with her. Ana played basketball with me until last year, but she wasn't on the team this year. I heard she was partying instead.

---

[54] Without an older sibling, I had no one to upgrade my musical taste; I was a slave to the trendy music on the radio and always would be.

Christmas lights already covered Ana's house, even though we hadn't celebrated Thanksgiving yet, and it looked like every light inside the house was on. There were cars everywhere. When I stepped onto the front door landing behind Don, it was obvious Ana's parents weren't home. The Clash blared "Rock the Casbah" at a volume that shook the windows of the split-level house, and I could see a grungy guy was mixing drinks upstairs in the kitchen. Ana's older brother held court in the living room; he obviously wasn't interested in enforcing rules, legal or otherwise. I could see more shadowy figures down the stairs in the darkened basement. Everyone had sloshy plastic cups in their hands. I didn't know if I should take off my coat or my electric blue shoes, but before I could decide Don took the stairs two at a time, up toward the light. I followed. Scott and Liz disappeared into the crowd.

Don mixed himself a drink from the assembled bottles and cartons on the kitchen counter. He scooped a few ice cubes from a drippy plastic bag on the counter. I read the label on the bottle from which glugged golden liquor: Rum. He topped it off with orange juice.

"Want some?" he asked.

"Can I taste yours?"

"Sure," he said, handing me his cup.

I took a swallow. It tasted like orange-flavored gasoline. I shuddered.

Don smiled. "Kinda strong, huh?"

"It's OK," I said.

Ana pushed through the crowd to us.

"I'm surprised to see you here," she said to me.

"Great party," Don said before I could answer. He moved through the crowd, and I followed. I knew some of the people standing around, but I never talked to them in school and I couldn't think of anything to say. Don mingled like a pro. I watched the music videos on TV. At one point, I took the cup out of his hand and had another gulp. I could see Scott looking at me from across the room, and I felt conspicuous. Other people looked at me like they didn't know what to say either.

After 38 Special's "You Keep Runnin' Away" aired, I glanced at Don with a look I hoped said, "Let's go." He picked up my signal, finished his drink and made for the front door.

When we emerged from the house, I felt like I could breathe again. Despite the ambient light from the house and the Christmas decorations, I could see stars twinkling in the sky. I felt relieved.

Scott and Liz didn't leave with us, so Don and I drove alone back to the high school cafeteria and the dance.

Jill quizzed me on where we had gone, who was there, and details of Don's behavior.

"I can't believe you went to Ana's party," Jill said, shaking her head. "I can't believe you drank."

Amy mutely looked at me with narrow eyes.

I didn't dance a single time all night.

+ + +

If the alcohol didn't tickle my fancy, it awakened my creativity:

> The rum and the beer, they've gone to my head.
> I'm dizzy, I'm drunk, my feet feel like lead.
> I can't talk, I can't walk, I can't even smoke.
> Everyone says, "What is this, a joke?"

+ + +

Just when I thought things couldn't get worse, Mr. Murphy's mock court reconvened on Monday. Mick got my hopes up when he testified in favor of the prosecution. Mick had a flair for the theatrical, and he effectively testified to George Gordon's motivation for killing Mrs. Magillacuddy. I guess I had briefed him well when we talked about it on the phone Sunday night. I was thinking about court, but Mick was thinking about something else, I guess.

"So, I know you like Scott Briller."

"Oh, yeah?"

"Yeah. Jill told me." Darn you, Jill.

"Well, practically everyone knows, I guess." Well, if Scott knows, he must hate me or something.

Mick's testimony at court on Monday wasn't effective enough. Or maybe *I* wasn't. Tonya had proven once again to be unbeatable. George Gordon was acquitted by the jury of our peers, and the state lost.

Holding hands with Scott was the best of November, but losing mock court was the worst. I had ended up prosecuting an innocent man *and* failing to land a boyfriend.

January 9, 1983

Dear Diary,

Valerie came to town with her boyfriend. They were touching and kissing the whole time. She seemed to want to rub it in. She got together with Scott Briller later on.

18

DECEMBER WAS A weird month. Excitement was promised like so many gifts under the tree; my birthday—my sixteenth birthday—was in December, and Christmas was coming. Merchants along Wadena's main street decorated their windows with gift-giving ideas accented with pine boughs and shiny ornaments. The Chamber of Commerce put up special street decorations and "welcome to Wadena" signs. Residents outlined the architectural features of their houses with multi-colored bulbs and festooned their pine trees with strings of sparkling lights. Driving around Wadena at night, especially when it was snowing, was an otherworldly experience. The outside world was happy, merry, happy, but I was stewing on the inside. I sucked at playing basketball, my parents seemed like they were suspicious of my every move after the party at Ana Arrowman's house (or maybe I was paranoid—how could they have found out?), and boys around every corner were ignoring me.

The first game in December, we played Perham. It was Parents Night so everyone played. I made two points and four fouls. I blocked[55] two girls on fast breaks.

Earlier, I filled time by watching Todd-the-God practice with the varsity basketball team. I sat on the bleachers, fiddling with the friendship pins on the bottom of my pants. Brent strolled by, sort of humming and singing, not usual at all. I don't know if he was singing for the heck of it or if he was trying to convey some sort of secret meaning, but he sang, "How I lost her, I don't know." Or something like that. Honestly, he was acting weird around me. As usual, he had me flummoxed.

After practice, Reeve Koroso gave Amy another dentist-white smile. It wasn't even for me, and my heart stopped like a bag of doughnuts after a double-cheeseburger meal.

Cindy decided to have a pizza party one Friday night. Amy and I were the only guests. We played Masterpiece with its thick cards of famous artwork and listened on the radio to the boys' basketball game in Breckenridge. I would have sacrificed a month of early curfews to go to the game. I knew Mr. President was there. At least I had heard he would be.

Cindy and Amy spent the evening trying to cheer me up because, on top of missing the basketball game, my cat ran away. Somehow, he got out of the house, and we couldn't find him anywhere. Dear K.C., who had saved me from Craig. I was afraid he'd freeze to death.

---

[55] My poor unsuspecting opponents were probably bruised the next day. When it came to fouls, I got my money's worth. I behaved more like I was playing hockey than basketball.

"Cats are smarter than dogs," said Amy, who had one of each at her house. I agreed. Sparky was loud, but barking was about all he was an expert at.

"He'll come back," Cindy said.

+ + +

My years as scorekeeper for boys' basketball led to a numerical discovery as to why I wasn't starting center. Amy was the high scorer among centers, and I had scored only two points all season. Even Christi Marans had seven points. I was horrified to think that Christi would start when Amy was gone to Florida.

Mom agreed to let me have my birthday party on December 12th, the Sunday before winter break and almost two weeks before my actual birthday. That way, Amy could be there before she left for Florida and it wouldn't conflict with everyone else's holidays.[56]

APPARENTLY, DAD WAS GOING FOR A CANDID SHOT OF ME, JILL, CINDY AND AMY HERE

---

[56] These are the trade-offs Christmas babies have to make.

Mom set the dining room table with her best china and lit candles. The Christmas tree lit up the corner of the room. Pretty lights and candles reflected in the glass windows surrounding three sides of the room. I curled my hair and dressed in a ruffled blouse and a flounced prairie skirt. Jill, Amy and Cindy arrived, and Dad took pictures. For dinner, Mom performed the role of server. Amy had helped me plan the menu. We had chicken and rice—my favorite—and side salads. Then, for dessert: Birthday cake. I hated traditional birthday cake, so Mom made cheesecake. Her version had a thin sour cream layer on top, and the whole thing was doused with cherry pie filling.

My friends sang happy birthday to me, and I was happy to be the center of attention. Then I opened my gifts. Amy gave me a backpack which I really needed. As I reflected on the evening later in the privacy of my bedroom I wrote, "Amy is my best friend. And I hers. We're closer than ever."

Christmas cards filled the mailbox every day. I wasn't interested in most of the letters because I didn't care where Mom's old college roommate was vacationing or how Dad's old classmates were bragging about their kids. But I liked the Christmas cards themselves, especially those with glitter, and I liked looking at people's pictures. One day, the Flourmans' Christmas card arrived in the mail and with it, a family photo. Brian, standing behind his mom with his brother, exuded handsome attitude; I imagined his eyes looking right at me. I pulled it out of Mom's pile of cards and showed it to Jill.

"Cute, huh?"

"Yeah, he is. Cuter than I expected."

I scoffed.

"Does he still have a girlfriend?" she asked.

"I have no idea." I rolled my eyes. Of course she would ask.

The second-to-last day before Christmas vacation, we played Aitken in Aitken. We came as close to winning a game as we ever had that season. The score was 29-25. Because of icy roads, we didn't get home until two o'clock in the morning. Amy had already left for Florida (and yes, Christi started instead of me), so I hung out all evening with Brenda and sat with her on the bus. She was the little sister to the Audio Concepts clerk with whom Amy had toyed. Before parting at 2 a.m., we agreed to go to a movie together the next week when Jill and Cindy would be skiing in Quadna Mountain Resort, the northern Minnesota version of Colorado. The next day, I had the personality of a zombie[57]. Christmas vacation never looked so good.

On the last day before break, we dissected frogs in biology. We were divided into groups, and I was teamed with Scott Briller, Jeff Ullman and Ana Arrowman[58]. Scott, ever the brain, did most of the dissecting. Thank goodness, because the whole enterprise made me want to barf. Once, when I was bent over, looking at something, Scott put his hand on the small of my back. A thrill shivered through me. It was pleasurable, but I was startled so I stood up, and he dropped his hand.

+ + +

Two days before my birthday, I get a letter in the mail from Amy.

---

[57] Back when zombies moved slowly and didn't growl.

[58] Ann was my second cousin so we shared a last name but beyond that, we had very little in common.

Monica,

How are you? I'm OK. This place is totally empty. The only people here are over 50![59] Hopefully, everybody will come later. Did you guys win? How's big Wadsville? Are you excited about being sixteen? Have any guys called you up saying "Please go with me!" Technically, you'll be eligible in two days.

I've been running every morning. Am I out of shape or what?

Do ya miss me? I miss you a lot. This will be the year I won't mind going home.

My mom's mood hasn't gotten better. Which doesn't bring my spirits up any. But I keep remembering what a great friend I've got and how nice Gary was the week before I left. Hopefully, I'll have something to look forward to in Wadsville, right?

Love, Amy

P.S. WRITE ME! Hope you pass your driver's test.

I got up early on my birthday, December 23. I was finally sixteen! I could officially date *and* drive. For the date, I needed a boyfriend, over which I had no control. But to drive, all I needed was my driver's license.

Waiting tormented me. I was a first-born, and that meant I sucked at waiting. People waited for me, maybe, but I never waited for anyone. Big, important events were *supposed* to happen on *my*

---

[59] Oh my God, they're practically dead!

schedule, not on God's[60]. It seemed I had waited forever to be able to drive. Waiting to attend driver's training classes. Sitting through boring movies about the horrors of trailing the car ahead too closely and not wearing seatbelts. Waiting for behind-the-wheel training. Languishing through Reeve Koroso's detailed descriptions of his summer jaunts to Mr. Pallid before I had my turn driving around the boring streets of Wadena. Accruing, in slow motion, enough hours of driving practice. Anticipating my birthday. Waiting for my name to be called to take my test. Sticking around for the results. All that waiting, just to get the chance to drive my parents' Crown Victoria to basketball practice and back.

Mom drove me to the court house at nine o'clock to take my driver's test. I passed with a 91. Poof! I was legal to drive. I breathed a sigh of relief.

If only I could pass the nonexistent boyfriend test so easily.

Grandma gave me a necklace and took me out for lunch at Dairy Queen. Grandma, my dad's mother, had been widowed for a decade, but she seemed utterly happy to be alone. She lived by herself in a small town fifteen miles away and filled her days with gardening, quilting and babysitting for the neighbors. I felt special that she came over to celebrate with me, especially since I would be seeing her the next night, Christmas Eve, when all my uncles and aunts and cousins filled her house with potluck casseroles and gifts.

Grandma insisted on driving to Dairy Queen. She probably didn't trust my driving skills yet, and I didn't either. While cars were passing Grandma and me on the highway in front of DQ, Brent and

---

[60] At least that's what I imagined at that point in my life. Boy, did I have some learning to do.

his brother rode by in the opposite direction and I smiled. I thought Brent waved, but I wasn't positive.

Mom gave me a subscription for *Women's Wear Daily* for my birthday. I had decided I didn't want to be a lawyer anymore—George Gordon cured me of that!—I wanted to be a fashion designer. But the best birthday present I could think of would be a date. Here I was, an old maid in tenth grade.

Christmas itself was a huge disappointment. I didn't get any clothes—gifts were the standard by which I measured holiday joy, and clothes were the best possible gift—except Mom and Dad gave me a bright red bathrobe. Where was I going to wear *that?*

Better than clothes, Mom and Dad let me borrow the car sometimes over Christmas break. As it turned out, they weren't the worst parents in the world. The other best gift I got: K.C. found his way home, skinnier than ever but otherwise OK. He was gone twenty-two days. I was so happy to have him snuggle my feet in bed again.

Since Amy was in Florida, and Jill and Cindy were skiing, all I did was go to basketball practice (like it helped) and play Intellivision. I didn't see Scott all vacation, except one night I dreamed he got his ears pierced; I hated guys with pierced ears. Besides the windshield wave with Brent, I saw him once after practice, but he didn't seem the least bit interested in talking to me.

An intriguing event took place during the boys basketball tournament, though. With Amy, Jill and Cindy all gone, I planned to keep official score on the sidelines and watch the other games with Kay when I was done. As was typical of my flighty sister, she wasn't even watching the game when I showed up. In desperation, I saw Royce

Koroso, with whom I had been shyly sharing smiles at our lockers all autumn, hanging out with his friends.

"Hey, can I hang out with you guys and watch the rest of the game?"

"Sure," Royce said, sort of noncommittally. But I saw his friend Greg elbow him.

Then Royce walked me home, and conversation flowed. It was a revelation. His brother, Mr. Perfect, had left me tongue-tied more times than I could count, and Royce's basketball teammate, Todd-the-God, rendered me mute by his mere presence. Royce, in contrast, asked me questions. And listened to my answers. I wowed myself by responding intelligently.

As I reflected on my year in my diary on New Year's Eve, I wrote: "Perhaps I underestimate my ability to converse with the opposite sex. I'm fat and getting fatter[61] but smart and getting smarter. I think I'm good-looking but no one else does. I wish I could be more popular. I'm not going to go as far as I did with Brian on my first date. That could/will mean trouble. I think I'm mellower than I was a year ago. I think I take life as it comes. I wish I had a boyfriend!!!"

---

[61] Oh, to be that "fat" again. Perhaps I was correct about "getting fatter," but I was not fat at age sixteen. I also wasn't as smart as I thought I was.

January 21, 1983

Dear Diary,

I am confused. Extremely confused. What a weird day.

Well, right before band Royce winked at me. Weak knees. I was happy.

Then I didn't see Royce all day. So after algebra (last block), I told Royce "good luck" with the game at Crosby-Ironton. He said "good luck" to me, too, but he said it like I was being a real pest. That made me sad.

Then I walked home with Amy and heard all her sob stories with Gary. It made me sadder.

Then we played Crosby Ironton at home. Amy played in all four quarters and I only played five or six minutes. It was an exciting game. We were behind all the way until the end. We tied 31-31 with about 1:30 left. Then someone fouled someone and they made a free throw. So we lost in the final seconds 32-31. And I was sure we were gonna win. We were gonna have a party afterwards. I was so saddened after the game I cried—honest-to-goodness cried. So I sat through pep band and Amy, Jill and Leslie and I went to Amy's for pop and cookies. Mom and Dad let me stay out until 11:30 so I could greet the boys coming home from Crosby. So we walked around a while. Then Ron Penny came along and we rode around until five minutes to 11. Ron dropped us off at the Junior High. I hoped to greet the boys and Royce, but the bus had already come and gone so only a few guys were left including Brent.

So Amy and I told him of our game, and I said I cried and he told us about his game. We were sad so Brent shook Amy's hand and then he hugged me. That made me HAPPY! And Amy mad!

But I was bummed about missing Royce. Now maybe Royce hates me. Now maybe Brent likes me. Then Amy would hate me. And Jill is having problems with Don and Beth. What will happen next? Tune in next time as "Monica Loves?"

19

WHEN SCHOOL RESUMED in January, *A Novel Idea* was waiting for me as usual on the top shelf of Jill's spotless locker, which had come to be our place of handing it off (no chance of Craig stowing an errant shoe in there!). By now, the progressive story was a thick sheaf of notebook paper. At some point, Amy had taped the holes of the first pages with masking tape so they would remain secure in the yarn binding. I shoved the pile in my English folder and hurried to class.

"Gah!" I gasped audibly when I read Jill's latest installment in which she killed off Gwendolyn's best friend Amber in a gas oven–related suicide while I was supposed to be reading a chapter in *Lord of the Flies*.

"I know what you mean," whispered Liz as she turned around with the book in her hands. Liz had been noticeably friendlier to me since we went to Ana Arrowman's party together. "I was shocked when they killed Simon, too. So disgusting."

"Oh my God, Simon dies, too?" I said.

"Too? You mean besides the pig?"

"The pig dies. Simon dies. Piggy dies. This is the most depressing story I've ever read," Mick said.

"What?! Stop talking!" I said. "I haven't gotten that far yet!"

"You'll be sorry when you do," Mick said solemnly.

"OK, that's enough, people, if you've finished reading, you can start outlining your summary," Mr. O said from the front of the room.

Liz returned to facing the front of the room, and I buried my head in my hands.

"You're killing me, Jill," I said at lunch.

"Um, no, I'm not killing *you*. I killed Amber," Jill said.

"Amber died?" Cindy said.

"Duh," Amy said. "The foreshadowing was obvious."

"How did you kill her?" Cindy said breathlessly and cracked her knuckles.

"That's not what I intended," I said. "What is this, *The Bell Jar*?"

"Actually, I don't think anyone actually dies in *The Bell Jar*," Jill says matter-of-factly. "The author did. Would you prefer that?"

"No." I shook my head and looked at Jill, trying to figure out if she was being stubborn or creative or only mean. "Why do you keep leaving me with these weird loose ends?"

"Life is messy," Jill said. "Listen, you wrote about the depressing stuff. I simply wrote Amber's story to its logical conclusion. If you want something specific to happen, then make it happen. You have a pen, too."

I was upset. Upset that Amber died. Upset that Jill made it happen. And upset that she was right. Jill took action while I dully waited for things to happen. In *A Novel Idea*, and in life, too. I had been fooling myself about being tired of waiting. Waiting was the natural consequence of not taking action.

"Listen, if you don't like it, you can write *A Novel Idea* by yourself," she said.

"Yeah, well," I said, sounding like I was in kindergarten, "maybe someday I *will* write a story by myself."

Reeve Koroso stopped me in the hallway and congratulated me on getting my driver's license. I tried to be cool, but inside, my eyebrows flipped over my head. I was flattered. I mean, I knew I wasn't about to get between him and his girlfriend—fat chance of that—but it was kind of him to remember that I turned sixteen.

Despite bonding a bit with Brenda on the 2 a.m. night of icy roads, I hated travel basketball games the most because I hated riding the bus. The way to the game was too noisy to do anything but talk, and the way home was either depressing (because we lost, again) or dark. Usually both. If I could manage it, I'd read a book and, one night on the bus, I started and finished "Waiting Games," a story about a girl named Jessie who fell in love with and got pregnant by Michael, her older guitar teacher and a member of The Skye Band. Jessie was only fourteen. "No big deal," I wrote in my diary. "I hated the ending though. I wished it could have been a happy ending."

When I got home one cold night in January, Mom and Dad called me into the living room. I usually got home from away basketball games after they went to bed, but they were still awake and watching TV.

"How was the game?" Mom asked.

"It was stupid," I said. "Amy was high scorer. I'm the No. 3 center. Amy is No. 1, Christi is No. 2 and I sat on the bench most of the game."

"Well, someone's got to keep the bench warm," Mom said. "You can't always be the best."

"That doesn't make me feel better," I mumbled.

"You could try harder. Run faster. Jump higher," Dad counseled. I rolled my eyes.

"Mrs. Palomino called us tonight," Mom said.

Questions raced through my mind. Why would Tonya Palomino's mom call my parents? Tonya wasn't playing basketball, and I hadn't hung out with her much since she kicked my butt in the George Gordon trial at Thanksgiving.

"It was about Craig," Dad said solemnly.

"Why does she care about Craig?" I said. "It's none of her business."

"Someone has been looking in Tonya's bedroom window at night," Dad said.

I stood silently in the living room, watching Johnnie Carson make jokes on "The Tonight Show" stage on the TV screen. It figured, I thought. Only Craig who rode his bike all winter would be a Peeping Tom during the coldest months of the year.

"Do you know if Craig ever looked in your window?" Dad asked.

"I don't know." I looked at the ceiling. What if he did and I never noticed? What if I didn't pull the shades when I got undressed at night? As creepy as it was to think of Craig seeing me naked, I wondered why he might be paying attention to Tonya now. The slut.

"Well, this behavior has to stop. I'm going to talk to Craig's parents tomorrow."

"Tonya never said anything to me," I said. I don't know why I was surprised. It's not like she would brag about it. "How does Mrs. Palomino know it was Craig?"

"She doesn't know for sure, but if it is, what's the next thing Craig will be doing?" Mom said.

"OK," I said, meekly. I was relieved Dad was going to take care of it, glad I didn't have to do anything.

"Craig needs help," Mom said.

"Do not talk to anyone about me talking to Craig's parents," Dad said sternly.

"OK." I turned and went to my room, shutting the door gently behind me. Why did Craig have to be so stupid, I wondered.

Dad went over to the Davidsons to talk to Craig's parents the next day. I bet Craig's face went white when my dad showed up at the front door.

Dad bawled out Craig's dad and laid down the law. "If you don't make sure this is the end of this, I'll go to the police." I assumed lots of yelling was involved.

"What did they say?" I asked when he got home.

"They took it OK," he said matter-of-factly, like he accused paramours of being Peeping Toms and underwear thieves every day. "They were going to talk to Craig as soon as I left."

I didn't know if I hoped Craig would get into trouble or not. I felt sorry for him. But I didn't feel sorry for Tonya.

Friday night, we won against Park Rapids. I played a half a quarter and didn't manage any stat-worthy actions. For the varsity game, I played cymbals in pep band until half time. Then Jill and I went over to Ela Baymont's house. Like Ana, Ela was a partier with a short elegant name and older brothers who could buy liquor. I was a partier now!

On the way over, I took a corner way too fast in Mom and Dad's Crown Victoria and ran over[62] a stop sign.

"What the hell are you doing?!" Jill said.

I pulled onto the shoulder and stopped.

"Oh my God, oh my God, oh my God." I gripped the steering wheel.

Jill hopped out, and so did I. Some guy was driving in the opposite direction. Surely, he must have seen what happened.

The stop sign was completely flattened. I had driven right over the top.

"Wow, I wonder if you damaged anything."

We looked back at the car, and everything seemed to be OK[63]. I crouched to look underneath, and nothing was hanging askew. Then I noticed it: A hub cab was missing.

"There it is!" Jill pointed it out in the gravel. I picked it up and tried to pop it back into place.

It worked.

Thank God.

"Let's go," I said, and we hopped back into the car and took off to Ela's. Neither of us would ever breathe a word about our accident but I felt naughty, guilty. Still, what could I do about it now?[64]

---

[62] Editor's Note: Not *into* or *through*? They bend over like that? Author's Note: Yes, *over*. Try it. You'll see. (No, wait, this is not a game of Truth or Dare.) Knocked it flat like it was an aluminum can, the "Stop" on its face looking up at the sky like it didn't know what hit it.

[63] Editor's Note: How can you hit a stop sign without damaging the car? Author's Note: My editor can't believe this. But it's true. Even things that were made like they used to be weren't made like they used to be. Unless they're Ford Crown Victorias. Then they're like bulldozers.

[64] Nothing. Except maybe have a drink.

Shortly after we arrived, Ana Arrowman and Tonya Palomino breezed in with Don, and we made the most of the available alcohol. I hated seeing Tonya, and the last topic of conversation I wanted to tackle was Craig, so we talked about alcohol: Where it came from, how much it cost, how to steal it from our parents and what types and brands tasted best. I thought they all tasted awful, but I didn't volunteer that opinion. I unadvisedly had a malt liquor, two aspirin and two glasses of Bacardi rum[65]. I felt woozy and light-headed. I'd never drunk that much before.

Then we went back to school to meet the guys coming back from their basketball game. I had two more aspirin. Somewhere, I'd heard aspirin packed a punch[66] and I believed it. I couldn't drive. Or at least, I felt like I shouldn't. I had done enough damage for one night. So Don drove, which was further evidence of my impaired decision making. I had hoped we could give Royce Koroso a ride home but his parents came and picked him up. So Jill and Don and I went cruising around in my car. We picked up Scott and Paul Tanqueray somewhere. We had neglected to stock our drinkware at Ela's house, so Don drove to some bar and grill in the country for some glasses. Then he drove to Oink Joint Road[67], a gravel turn-off the main highway where a handful of teenagers—some I knew, some I didn't— had already gathered. In the summertime, we would be hidden on this road by corn fields, but a layer of snow covered the fields now.

---

[65] Malt liquor is beer with a higher alcohol content. It should never be consumed in conjunction with pain killers of any kind (including aspirin) and definitely not at the same time as one drinks rum of any brand. No matter what your age.

[66] If by "punch," the ubiquitous *they* meant mixing pain relievers and alcohol liquefies your liver, then yes, it packs a punch. Don't try this at home.

[67] This real name of a road near Wadena is so good I couldn't have made it up.

While everyone else was finishing off the Bacardi, Jill walked me around trying to sober me up. The gray snow and the gray night sky melted together; I concentrated on putting one blue-shoed foot in front of the other. I was exaggerating my haze, not wanting to let on that I was fully aware, just unsteady. I knew I didn't want to have more to drink, and screwing around half dizzy seemed like reasonable cover, but later I realized I had made a complete fool of myself.

At 11:30 p.m., we dropped off the boys and Jill brought me home and tucked me into bed. When I filled in Dear Diary the next day, I wrote, "I was so bombed."

I liked being drunk but I didn't like the person I became drunk. I couldn't handle myself. That was the first time I'd consumed enough alcohol to affect my behavior. I vowed not to do that again.

Saturday, I went to the hoop shoot to talk with Royce and Brent and any other boys who might be there. That night, I told Mom and Dad I was going to the movies. Instead, Jill and I went over to Don's house. Then Jill, Don's little brother, Don and I cruised around in his car. After a bit, we left Don's little brother home alone and went back to the bowling alley where we met Ana. We were in my Crown Victoria now which had plenty of room for more trouble. It was like adding seats to the game musical chairs instead of subtracting them. Don suggested we pick up Brent and two of his friends.

I apologized to one of them for my behavior at Ela's house the night before.

"Yeah, I heard," Brent said. "Can't handle your liquor, huh?"

"It'll never happen again," I said, literally and emotionally sober. I intended to stay that way.

Eventually, we dropped off Ana, then one of Brent's friends, then the other. While we were driving around, I took another left-hand turn too fast, and I saw my poor Crown Victoria's hub cab rolling around the snow-packed street in my rearview mirror.

"Gadzooks[68]!" Brent, who was sitting next to me in the front seat, looked down at his hands, shook his head and said "shit" under his breath, like he'd never heard a girl swear before. That dumb loose hub cap preoccupied me more than my unladylike language. As before, I stopped the car, retrieved the hub cap, wedged it back in place and took off. I hoped it would stay on this time.

Jill and Don were alone in the back seat. We were a quartet. I had already missed my curfew, but I didn't want the night to end.

Brent made conversation by talking about Shelley Anson and Liz Sullivan, whom he wanted to ask out.

"But I can't drive yet," he said more than once.

I saw through his excuse of lacking a license. What he actually lacked was courage. He was afraid of rejection. It wasn't appealing that he was lusting after other girls, but I saw an opening for me in the moment because he was in the car I was driving.[69]

I found a dead end near Brent's house and parked. Jill and Don stayed in the back seat while Brent and I got out. It was strangely quiet after listening to 1982 disco at top volume on the radio. The air was cold but still; it was relatively bearable for a winter evening in Minnesota. A full moon hung in the sky, and a street light nearby cast a glow over us.

"So I guess I still owe you two kisses for making fourteen points in a game in eighth grade, huh?" I said.

---

[68] Only I didn't say "gadzooks," I used a much angrier and vulgar word my mother might use to describe a method by which women get pregnant.

[69] A bird in the hand is worth two in the bush. In other words, a boy in the car is worth two bushes.

"Yeah, you do. And one more for when you bet I couldn't hit a telephone pole with a snowball."

"I don't remember that bet," I said.

"I do."

"Well, I'm willing to pay up."

I leaned back against the front end of the car, and Brent stood so close I could smell his breath and see the hairs on his chin. I saw tentative hunger in his green eyes, and his full lips looked inviting. He leaned in and tried to French kiss right away.

I pulled back and looked him in the eye.

"I didn't say *French* kisses."

"You didn't *not* say French kisses."

Like a hen, I pecked him on the lips three times only I lingered on the third one and he held me tight. We French kissed for a moment, but he aggressively inspected my mouth rather than savored it. He wasn't as good a kisser as Brian Flourman. It was pleasant, but somehow it didn't measure up to the kiss in fantasies that came as the culmination of years of flirtation and desire.

"I've got to get home," I said.

"Me, too. I guess."

We climbed back into the car where Jill and Don separated lips briefly, and I drove Brent home. Then I dropped off Don, then Jill.

I parked the car in my garage, and sneaked into the house as quietly as I could. The clock in the kitchen read 12:14.

January 28, 1983

Dear Diary,

Kay's having a slumber party downstairs right now so I'll write in you because I'll probably not get to sleep anyway. Besides, a lot happened today.

Amy is/was sick today so on the bus to Detroit Lakes, I sat with Brenda. She told me she got two incompletes last quarter. I would never do that.

Royce smiled and winked at me in lunch today. It made me happy. After school he came to my locker to talk to me and exchange trivialities about wishing each other good luck on our respective games.

Well, I guess I was thinking about Royce too much because at D.L. I was not mentally prepared for the game. I knew I was gonna start and Tonya psyched me out. Anyway, it was the worst game I've ever played. I couldn't catch the ball for anything and I was stuffed about a billion times. I didn't make any points—few rebounds. And the worst of all—I made four fouls in the first two quarters. We were losing bad by the end of second quarter, and I felt sad so I was crying. Bonnie was sitting next to me and she gave me a pep talk but when I started second half, I was still so screwed I couldn't do anything right. WHAT A BUMMER!!!

20

THE MORNING AFTER I stayed out too late French kissing with Brent, Mom was mad. Really mad.

"I heard what time you got home," she said while clanging breakfast dishes around the kitchen. "Your father is none too pleased either."

Good thing he didn't know about the hub cap, I thought.

No more was said until after church. Dad didn't seem too steamed, which was unnerving. Usually, he was the one stomping around, yelling with an edge in his voice that made me cringe.

"We're not going to punish you for missing curfew this time, but this is the last time you'll get to go out twice in one weekend."

"Whaddaya mean?! I didn't do anything wrong. I'm trustworthy," I lied.

"You can't use that 'I'm trustworthy, I'm responsible' line again," he said. "You knew what time you were supposed to be home, and you weren't. It's as simple as that. Don't argue with me."

So, let's see, I had succeeded in disappointing Scott and everyone who saw me drunk on Friday. I managed to tick off Jill, who had to tuck me into bed. I probably turned off Brent by coming on too strong and leaving too quickly. And now my parents thought I was irresponsible and untrustworthy. Great. Just great.

I stayed home from school on Monday. I was coming down with a cold, and if I had gone, I would have had to go Fergus Falls for our basketball game, and then I would have been up late, and I knew I would be *actually* sick the next day[70]. Besides, Mr. O didn't need me anyway. Christi was No. 2 now and I was No. 3. Sick and uncoordinated—I wantonly added those to my stack of troubles.

School on Tuesday was awkward. Mick told me everyone was shocked to hear about me getting drunk on Friday. Who told Mick, I wondered. The truth came out.

"Everyone on the boys basketball team was talking about it on the bus yesterday," he said, repeating the prattle. "'Monica Wallgren?! Drinks?!'"

"Yeah, I guess she does," I said. "What a dummy."

I thought again of what I said when Scott was ushering me out of his house the night I played Dig Dug at the bowling alley with Jill and he held my hand: "Whatever you guys want, just don't make me a part of it all." Why had I said that when I clearly must have wanted to become "a part of it all"? If I found Scott's smoking and drinking appalling, why did I want him to like me? I was confused, but I knew I didn't like myself much anymore. I had dared to move out of my comfortable nerdy-girl box, and the experiment was an utter failure.

Brent did everything but skip classes to avoid me. I didn't know what to think. Was he embarrassed about kissing me Saturday night? Grossed out? Talk about one-night stands.

---

[70] I could predict all *these* eventualities but I was incapable of foreseeing anything related to my love life.

+ + +

After losing our game against Staples on Thursday thanks to what I described in my diary as a couple of "really shitty refs" (I scored a point though), I looked forward to keeping stats for the ninth-grade boys game against Staples on Friday and watching the tenth-grade game.

The ninth graders, with Todd-the-God and a lot of other talent, including Reeve Koroso's little brother Royce, won several games during the season, including this one. Royce's athletic skill was nothing compared to Todd's deity-like ability to handle the ball and peel off winning jump shots, but I noticed how Royce towered over everyone else on the court. He was listed as 6-foot-3 in the program.

When the tenth graders played without interlopers from other grades, they lost. Always. Brent was an aggressive ballplayer with sticky hands, and when he came off the bench in varsity games, he was great, but as a group, the tenth-grade boys sucked.

That night, however, they won. The first honest-to goodness win since seventh grade. It was such an exciting game and even better because they beat Staples, Wadena's arch rival. By the end of the game, the sparse crowd of fan-girls (including me) and parents in the gym were on their feet, jumping up and down and yelling sentiments of congratulations.

Brent played like a pro. In the hallway after the game, I congratulated everyone including Mick, Craig and Scott. I wanted to hug Brent with his huge smile, but he was a sweaty mess.

"Maybe I was a good luck charm," I said. "Maybe we should do more often what we did last Saturday."

Brent simply smirked.

While I was watching the varsity game, Scott sat behind me in the bleachers. He played with the hair on my neck, which sent tingly shivers down my spine, and I sensed he sniffed my head—he clearly had a thing for hair. Oh, thank goodness for my Fabregé Organics Shampoo with pure wheat germ oil and honey[71]. Boy, was I glad I deep conditioned that morning! I wanted to turn around, but I didn't. I hoped my body language was saying, "yes, yes, yes!"

After the varsity game, I stood in the hallway with Scott and a bunch of other boys. Girl after girl walked up to Scott and congratulated him and hugged him including, of course, Tonya Palomino, Ana Arrowman and Ela Baymont. Was I jealous? Did he like it? I didn't know.

After a few minutes, I donned my winter gear for the walk home. Amy and Jill planned to go to the Blue Hor[72] to listen to the band Fury. Fury was Amy's sister's boyfriend's band. Amy had met the lighting guy at some point, and she had a thing for him, now that Gary Boot was ignoring her. He was charming and rich but not cute, she said. Supposedly, he liked her, too. But I had to go home because Mom and Dad refused to let me go out after being late last weekend. Oh, if they only knew.

I replayed the events of the past week and the night in my mind on the way home. Brent was annoying; I could never tell where I stood with him. He could have Shelley or Liz or whomever he thought he had to have before we kissed in the moonlight. But Scott. Hmm, Scott was mysterious. And tall. And he liked my hair. Before

---

[71] I had no idea why "organic" was important and only a vague notion of wheat germ, but it made my hair smell good.

[72] The bar's real name was the Blue Horizon, but no one called it that. The "blue horizon" it was invoking on the edge of the wintry prairie could only have been northern lights, not a watery Caribbean vista.

he was assaulted by all the hugging girls in the hallway, Scott grabbed my hand, and clasped it between both his hands, like he was making a pact. "In two or three weekends, we will go and party and have some whiskey," he said.

I will *live* for two or three weekends from now, I thought. I will be on my best behavior so Mom and Dad can't ground me. I want to stay out late and party!

When I got home, I listened to a rebroadcast of the boys basketball game on the radio. Then I switched it to FM and hit the sleep button. John Cougar's "Jack and Diane" came out of the tinny radio speakers. As I closed my eyes to go to sleep, I thought of Brian. How he kissed me. How erotic it felt.

Jill's soap opera with Don went from crummy to intolerable. Or from crummy to wonderful to crummy again. I didn't know. All I knew was she was Unhappy and Upset with capital "U's."

Amy had a great time at the Blue Hor, Jill reported when she called me Saturday night. Both of us were restricted to home, so we relied on the phone to catch up.

John, the lights man, was all over Amy, Jill said. And Amy liked him, too, Jill guessed, based on how much they were tongue wrestling.

"Nice," I said, both repulsed, as I imagined Amy kissing John, and intrigued.

"Yeah, did you know he called her twice long-distance[73] last week?" Jill said.

---

[73] These were the days long before unlimited minutes. You could talk to a local boy as long as your dad would let you, but when you were interested in someone far away? Sweet nothings over the phone cost you dearly.

"No, she must have missed telling me that." Somehow, between kissing Gary on her first date and getting long-distance phone calls from cute lighting guys, she had stopped trusting me with her secrets.

"Well, it was dumb. I don't know why I went with her. She didn't need me."

"Bummer."

"Missy Keskikallio called me. She was at the speech meet today with Don, and she told me Beth came home, and Don made everything alright with her. Can you believe that?"

"Oh, no!"

"I was going to go to the speech meet, but I didn't. I should have. I can't believe Don didn't tell me."

"What a bummer." I was running out of comforting things to say.

"So, do I act like I don't know, or what?"

"I don't know."

"Do you think he got back together with Beth because I went to the Blue Hor with Amy?"

"I doubt it. He wouldn't do that."

"I don't care. He's a jerk anyway. And Beth's a bitch. He deserves her."

She was lying. I knew she cared. I was sad for her.

We talked more than an hour. About Don. About Amy. About Brent. About Scott. About kissing Brent. About holding hands with Scott. Jill called me a sex monger.

"I wrote a poem about you," she said.

"Read it to me."

> Mileage Monica is never boring.

Her man won't have time for snoring!

"It's true!" I said. I loved Jill's sense of humor, even when she was feeling down. "That's hilarious!"

+ + +

Jill eventually cornered Don and talked it out. Sort of. Don, full of conflicting impulses and loyalties, decided to stick with Bitchy Beth. I decided I hated Beth for asserting her power and snatching Don away from Jill.

Scott had me doubting myself. He didn't mention anything all week in biology class about partying. What if he didn't want me along anymore? What if he had decided my stupidity trumped my awesome hair?

I tried to rationalize Scott's silence about our party date. He partied every weekend so he wouldn't talk about it every day, right? He had been in biology with me all year, so he knew what I was like and he was still talking to me.

On the other hand (or maybe the third hand by now), I had changed. I wasn't a goody-two-shoes anymore. I felt guilty about so many things. I wished I hadn't gotten drunk. I was sorry I ran over that sign (but I was grateful Dad never found out).

Then Jill dropped a bombshell on me. After she dropped me off on Friday, she went to Scott's to play pool and hang out. Scott told her he liked my character but hated me drunk. Liked my character?! Hated me drunk?! I hated me drunk, too. I couldn't do it again. But who was Scott to judge me?

And every time I thought about kissing Brent, I got the chills, just like with Brian. What if I had bad breath? Or I did it all wrong? And that's why he hadn't talked to me for almost two weeks?

+ + +

The night I was supposed to party with Scott and drink whiskey ended in soggy disappointment.

He never talked to me about it on the days leading up to his promised date, but I still held out hope that I would see him after the basketball game and could ask to go along. I planned to drink but not get drunk.

I talked to Don at the game, and he said he was going to meet up with Scott later. At least that's what he *said*. I asked him if I could tag along, and he said, "Sure." He was going to meet everyone else at the Cozy Theater at 9:30.

The Cozy Theater was an icon in Wadena. The historic building sat on a high-traffic corner on Main Street. The art deco marquee lined in lights touted the movie of the week on the theater's only screen.

So I showed up at 9:30. It was snowing that sort of heavy wet snow that wilted my hair as effectively as rain. I imagined people inside enjoying the velvet seats and buttery popcorn. No one on the street even resembled Don or anyone else I knew. I had been played for a fool, and it stung.

So I walked to Amy's house.

"I've got to use your curling iron," I said when she greeted me on her porch.

"Huh? My curling iron?"

"Yeah, the snow wrecked my hair—look at it! It's horrible!"

I pushed my way in and realized John, the band groupie who ran the lightshow, was there. He looked perturbed that I'd shown up in the middle of his evening with Amy. Too bad, I thought. Whose night was ruined here?

I stomped straight to the bathroom to perform my hair repairs. In the family room, Amy and John exchanged giggly whispers, apparently deciding to drive to Perham. I didn't know why. Maybe the band was there? So they dropped me off at the bowling alley on their way out of town.

Tonya and Shelley were at the bowling alley. I didn't normally spend time with Shelley even though her mom invited me to Shelley's surprise birthday party, but I wasn't looking for anyone specific—I was looking for *anyone*. Tonya and Shelley were convenient. We walked to the Pizza Dena (thank goodness it had stopped snowing). If the pizza joint had a sound track that night, it was a bassline of boredom with a melody of isolation. Tonya talked to her ex-boyfriend. She was nice to him, but I didn't understand why. When you broke up, shouldn't you hate each other? I saw Gary Boot, and he briefly made conversation with me. This bewildered me because after his fling with Amy, I didn't think he ever even noticed me.

Eventually, Scott walked through the glass door of the pizza shop. His eyes met mine, and he knew I knew he had ditched me. I smiled a fake wide grin he couldn't miss from across the room. I was disappointed to the point of crying, which I would not do in public. I said goodbye to Tonya and Shelley, who barely noticed, and I pushed my way through the crowd which squirted me out into the street with its soggy piles of snow. I picked my way through the melting snow and ice to home.

In my mind, I sorted through my conflicting feelings about Scott. Scott was such a dink. Just because I was so pure, it meant I couldn't party?! I came on too strong, I thought. I was too eager. Too eager to get drunk again. So Scott could get A grades and get drunk every weekend, but I couldn't. Was that it? What a hypocritical, arrogant dink.

About halfway home, I caught a glimpse of Scott driving around in his parents' Lincoln Continental. If he saw me, he didn't stop. I hated him. I hated him because I knew he hated me. I decided that night would be the last night I would ever curl my hair. Out of protest. Scott was a dink, and I was going to be a rebel.

Maybe I liked Brent, I thought.

When I got home, Mom and Dad were in bed. I hadn't missed my curfew, but the house was dark. I turned on the portable TV in the kitchen nook, and flipped the channel to "Friday Night Videos." I found some edible leftovers in the fridge and created a weird, towering sandwich of meatloaf, spaghetti noodles, leftover squash, cheese, lettuce and mustard. After I ate it, I felt full but I was still empty inside. So I made cinnamon toast with lots of butter and sugar for dessert.

I sat glumly in the kitchen staring at the linoleum, feeling woozy from all the carbohydrates and listening to "Friday Night Videos." All the songs were dumb. I felt like a pig. I was worthless.

What a shitty night. Period. End of story.

February 28, 1983

Dear Diary,

After weightlifting today, I went over to the boys B-ball practice. I talked to Scott while he was stretching out. I don't remember all that we talked about but it was a good conversation.

Friday I'm gonna go to a party at Royce's. Don will be there. I guess I have to be a "host" for the A game that's gonna be played here. But that should go fast. I think it's Friday anyway—the party, I mean. I mentioned it to Mom & Dad. They have to let me stay out late. I'm gonna have fun.

Amy walked home with Sam Anderson. Wow!

Jill talked to Don. Sort of. Poor Don. And I hate Beth!

I just finished watching the last episode of M*A*S*H. It will go down in history.

Brent talked to me today. Wonder of wonders!

I'm a sex monger. Jill agrees with that.

I smiled at Royce in the hallway today. He said, "Hi."

March 6, 1983

Dear Diary,

I'm in the spring play. I will be a dumb shepherd.

21

I WAS SO PSYCHED for a party with Scott, I almost forgot about the winter seasons dance. I had planned to skip it—what was the point?—but Jill talked me into it. I asked Mom to braid my hair because I'd committed to not curling it.

"Well, who do you hope to dance with tonight?" she asked.

"No one. I won't dance. I know it."

"Not with that attitude," she said.

"Maybe Brent will dance with me, but he's not talking to me right now, so probably not."

"Why isn't he talking to you?"

I wasn't about to tell Mom he wasn't talking to me because I was a terrible kisser, so I lied.

"He's a dink."

"I see."

"Maybe Royce Koroso will dance with me," I said. "He hung out with me at the basketball game a couple weeks ago."

"Maybe you should ask him."

"No way," I said. "He's 6-foot-3, you know."

"No, I didn't know. I guess I'm not paying attention."

"So he's taller than I am."

"Perhaps you should pay more attention to how pleasant someone is to you rather than how tall he is."

"Mom, if you haven't noticed, I'm freakishly tall." Everyone else was into clogs, but they all had too much heel; I wore my flat blue shoes everywhere for a reason. Mom could be so dense sometimes.

"You know, height doesn't matter in bed," said my matter-of-fact mother who, at 5-foot-3, was nearly a foot shorter than my father.

"What?!" I shrieked, looking at my mother in the mirror.

Later, when I told Jill what my mom said, she looked at me in horror. "Your mother really said that?!"

"Really."

"Did she mean …?"

"I don't know what she meant. I'm only telling you what she said."

Amy came to the dance because she wasn't much interested in John anymore. *I* would have rather gotten wasted. Fat chance of that. Scott talked to me—shocker—but he didn't ask me to dance. And I heard Don (who, by the way, was treating Jill like he did before Beth came back) say that he wanted to get fried, but he didn't offer me any invitations to nearby parties, either.

Turned out, going to the basketball tourney with Royce and his friends a few weeks before was the best dance move I ever made because both his friends each asked me to dance, *and* Royce danced with me three times. The first time he asked me to dance, he strode straight across the cafeteria to me and said, "Can I have this dance?" Impressive.

One of the times he asked, it was a slow dance! Really impressive!

Slow dancing with Royce blew my mind. First of all, I could put my arms beneath his because he was so much taller than I was. And I could rest my head on his shoulder. He put his hands on my back and held me close like I might fall without him. It was overwhelmingly sexy. And he had asked the deejay to dedicate the dance to us. Royce was considerate in such a sincere and romantic way. And then he walked me home! Like before, our conversation dipped into a number of subjects, and we never ran out of things to say.

After years of going to dances and being disappointed at the lack of movement in my love life, a dance had finally made a difference.

By Monday, I couldn't wait to see Royce. When he winked at me between classes, my knees almost buckled. After school, I walked Jill almost all the way home, not because I didn't want her walking alone but because I had ulterior motives—she lived only a block from Royce. My detour panned out. We saw Royce and his friends, and we stood in the street talking for almost an hour. Royce's friends were friendly, not jerks like Brent-the-Cheese and Scott-the-dink.

I decided I truly liked Royce. I couldn't quite explain it, but he was special. He tried so hard to be a clever conversationalist, and he was. I liked that he seemed interested in me. The real me.

But anxiety filled every wrinkled crack in my brain. He invited me to a party at his house. I didn't know what to expect. I mean, Valerie Stonyridge's party in eighth grade was ages ago, but boy-girl parties still worried me. I feared—was embarrassed by—kissing. The music playing, someone throws out a dare or spins a bottle, and then what would happen?

Here was the other source of anxiety: What might happen *after* kissing? I shuddered, thinking about how Brian tried to get in my pants. Maybe it was guilt that made me shudder so. But being sinful wasn't the worst of it. Kissing had real-life consequences, not just spiritual ones. Tonya had been spreading a rumor about Valerie recently: That Valerie was pregnant. When I heard it, I silently denied the gossip, but I knew it could be true. Valerie was reckless. I saw how her boyfriend touched her at the football game the autumn before, how hungry he looked. That Valerie would do more than kiss didn't surprise me. But I also knew enough about birth control to wonder how Valerie could have gotten pregnant. Her uninhibitedness didn't seem fearless and daring, it seemed weak and wanton.

It'll turn out alright, I reasoned. I hope? I was apprehensive. Kissing was always hardest the first time.

Friday, March 18, 1983

Dear Diary,

I had a pretty good day schoolwise. And I bowled a 116 in gym. And I wrote a great poem in Algebra. But ...

Jill was talking to Brent today. She said he said he didn't even want to think about that night. Boo hoo! And I liked it! Fag!

Wayne Nelson accused me of brown-nosing Al Lynk, the director of our play. I don't want that. I'll have to be lethargic from now on.

I babysat tonight. So tomorrow night Jill and I are going out. I hope we have fun.

22

AT THIS POINT IN my life, I believed two things: That every problem had a solution—somewhere, somehow—I just had to find it. I must have learned this from Dad. He could fix anything, and I mean *anything*. He even repaired my hot rollers once[74]. Before I was born, he was tinkering with room-sized computers for Control Data Corp., and then he taught others the ones and zeros of electronics at Wadena Tech School. By now, he co-owned the Wadena TV Center. After supper, which my Mom always had on the table promptly at five o'clock, he often went back to work. The only evening the TV Center was open was on Thursdays, but on other evenings when the sign out front was dark, he huddled over a broken television carcass in the back room, figuring out why there was no picture or no sound or why there were lines across the screen or no power or any number of other problems that plagued electronic items back then[75]. He called these after-work stumpers "dogs." "Oh, I've got two dogs I

---

[74] Twice actually. Why throw a set of hot rollers away when you have a dad who can fix anything?

[75] When fixing electronics was still cheaper than replacing them.

can't figure out right now. Something is wrong with the transient-voltage-suppression diode in one of them, I think. A real dog. I've got to work it out. I'll be home soon." Invariably, he *would* work it out, repair the transient thingy whatsy and please another customer. That's how I thought the world worked, too. With enough time and persistence (and, usually, advice from a book), every problem could be solved. That's how I figured out Rubik's Cube over the summer, and throughout my life I would turn to books[76] every time I faced a dog, whether a puzzle or an emotional quandary.

And the second article of my teenage faith: That my life would be better if I had a boyfriend.

Royce looked like a reasonable prospect for "boyfriend." But, like a masked intruder, the whole kissing problem kept me awake at night. I might know how to *be kissed,* but I didn't really know anything about *kissing.* As had been clearly demonstrated with Brent, my kissing experience left something to be desired.

After the boys basketball game on Friday, Royce and his friend Greg walked me home again. When we were standing in my driveway—with poor Greg looking on, I kissed Royce on the cheek and walked straight into the house. I didn't even look back to see his expression.

It was only his cheek. But I hoped he liked it.

The next day, I shaved and masked and primped and curled all day to prepare for the party at Royce's house. When I arrived, he led me down the basement steps into the low-ceilinged dark. Music emanated from an expensive boom box in the corner at a volume certainly dictated by Royce's mother upstairs. I don't remember the

---

[76] And, later, Google.

particulars of the social interactions that night, but they didn't include terror-inducing truth-or-dare games. Near the end of the evening, I sat on the sofa and Royce put his extra-long arm around me. He felt warm and strong and shy, but his touch made me feel like I was giggling on the inside. And he walked me home. He always did. He was such a gentleman. He wasn't like Brent. Royce *wanted* to spend time with me.

When we got to my driveway, I asked him if I embarrassed Greg the night before, and Royce said, "No." He laughed. Royce had a chuckle that sounded like chunky ice cubes falling from a happy ice machine.

"So, do I get a kiss back tonight?" I couldn't believe I asked.

"Absolutely."

Royce stepped close, and I looked up into his eyes—up!—and he leaned in. I was wearing my favorite blue shoes, and Royce stood a solid five inches taller than I did. Then, disaster! I didn't know which way to turn my head, and we bumped noses. I kept going in anyway, determined to make it happen, and our lips touched the way they're supposed to, but it was awkward. I tried to smooth it over. I smiled, and said good night, but I left the fumbled kiss hanging in the air.

Real kissing was not like in the movies, all romantic music and perfectly executed meeting of the lips. Real kissing was messy. "Bad breath" had never entered my mind until I saw Brian buy 7up before he made out with me the first time. And then it was all teeth and tongue and scratchy and wet. Oh, the tongue! If I thought long enough about tongues, they became slimy, muscular, disgusting snails, but when I closed my eyes and remembered Brian's tongue, I got hot and my heart beat faster.

So kissing was romantic, too, but Royce and I were stuck in the middle of messy and poorly executed.

He called me on Sunday and asked me to go to the movies, but I couldn't go because it was a "school night," stated by Dad without opportunity for argument. Still, I was thrilled because A) He called me even though our kiss was stupid, and B) Going to the movies would be a date! My first date! I was asked on my first date! I was 16 now, and I could accept!

On Monday, when I was supposed to be researching scientific studies about the safety of phenylalanine (otherwise known as aspartame) which was showing up in soda pop[77] of all flavors at the time, I spent an entire period in the library looking up kissing. After my encounter with Brian, I thought I knew what I was doing, but boy, was I wrong. *Brian* knew what he was doing; I was in no position to lead on this task. I needed more information so I did what would become a lifelong habit when I encountered a problem I couldn't solve—I went to the experts, preferably sources that couldn't talk back. I was surprised to find dozens of magazine articles[78] on the subject. I also copied the definition of "love" out of the dictionary:

> **love** (luv), **n., v.,** **loved, loving,** —n. **1.** A strong or passionate affection for a person of the opposite sex. ...
>
> — **Syn. 1.** LOVE, AFFECTION, DEVOTION, all mean a deep and enduring emotional regard, usually for another person. LOVE may apply to various kinds of regard: the charity of the Creator, reverent adoration toward God or toward a person, the relation of parent and child, the regard of friends for each other, romantic feelings for one of the opposite sex, etc., AFFECTION is a fondness for persons of either sex, that is enduring and tender, but

---

[77] Or simply "pop" as it's known in Minnesota.
[78] This was a high school library, people.

calm. DEVOTION is an intense love and steadfast, enduring loyalty to a person; it may also imply consecration to a cause.

After basketball practice that afternoon, I returned home to learn that Brian Flourman had been to the house.

"Brian Flourman stopped by for you," Mom said without looking at me. She lifted a lamp on the end table to dust underneath it.

I stood in the middle of the living room, looking at her. Brian lived four hours away. Why had he been here?

"For me?"

"He said he'd stop by another time. She was humming. I never understood how she could be happy when she was housecleaning.

Part of me was glad I missed Brian. I quietly freaked out. Why was Brian looking for me? And what would Royce say?

I didn't tell Mom any of this. As I walked to my bedroom, I heard her singing under her breath: "Why must I be a teenager in love?"

Royce's skills with geometry were like Albert Einstein's skills with a curling iron. Like most every other class, geometry came easily to me. Perimeter of a rectangle equals length times width. Area of a circle equals pi times radius squared. The length of the hypotenuse squared is equal to the length of side A squared and the length of side B squared. First comes love, then comes marriage, then comes what? I preferred complicated geometrical formulas to complex relationship puzzles.

So as we warily learned more about each other, we studied geometry together for two hours one evening. Really studied. We had our heads together over his geometry book, and he turned to face me, and he said he liked me. Imagine that! Royce liked me even though I was brainy! I looked right into his eyes, and I smiled. And then I said something about properties of parallelograms. And then Royce walked me home, just like always. But just like always, he sort of hemmed and hawed when it came time to kiss goodnight.

Finally, I couldn't stand it anymore. I kissed the inside of my fingers and touched his lips. "See ya tomorrow," I said.

When I got in the house, I was a half hour late. I overheard Mom and Dad fighting about me and the decisions they made about me. I heard Mom complain about me having friends over all the time who ate all her food, but I surmised Mom wanted to give me more freedom and Dad was upset about this. Dad didn't believe we actually studied for two hours! Diary summary of the situation: "Sick! We did! Dad was stupid! Sick."

I didn't care what MomandDad thought. I liked studying with Royce. Maybe tomorrow I would give him a kiss for each right answer he gets, I thought. That would be casual.

I got an unfamiliar fizzy feeling in my stomach like I drank pop too fast every time I thought about Royce. He was different than anyone else. He honestly liked me—he said so! He wasn't only trying to get in my pants like Brian. He appreciated my intelligence and apparently liked how I kissed, unlike Brent. And unlike Scott, I didn't have to puzzle out why his actions didn't match his words. Royce liked me and he said so.

Thursday, March 24, 1983

Dear Diary,

Today at play practice (school play), David Green was there. We talked for 30 seconds about Brent and how that was history and he said, "So now who's the lucky guy?" Imagine—he said lucky! And he was talking about me!

23

STUDYING—WHETHER IT was geometry or kissing—didn't help much. Royce got a 23 out of 40 on the geometry test. Mr. Svensson in geometry obviously liked me and made me feel smart. I wished he could do the same for Royce. As was typical for me when I got bored in class, I used my time for creative writing. I wrote Royce a poem:

> I'm drowning in geometry,
> And no one even cares.
> It's not like there's a pool in here,
> And I can't breathe the air.
> It's like, I have so much to do
> I'll never get it done.
> I'll work, I'll sweat, I'll toil hard.
> I'll wish: Away I'd run.
> And then he says, "Clean off your desks."
> And hands out three white sheets.
> On the top of Number 1
> It says "Test." I can't even cheat.

> I take the test and get a D,
> Which stand for "drown," you see.

At the girls varsity basketball game, I sat with Amy. No one else was sitting near us when Brent walked into the gym, sauntered up the bleachers and sat beside me. Which was great. But then Royce walked in, and I wanted him to sit with me so I waved him over, and he sat down between me and Amy. That must have embarrassed Brent because he moved almost right away. I liked Brent, but I liked Royce, too. The Cheese stands alone.

Amy, who got her driver's license on her birthday, drove Royce and me home in her Chevette. Well, it wasn't literally *her* Chevette, but it was the car her parents let her drive. She gave Royce's friend Greg a ride home, too, and she even let him drive part of the time. He didn't even have his driver's license yet! I would never do that. What if he had an accident? Nonetheless, we had a fun time.

Amy called me later and told me she thought Greg was neat. But it turned out to be irrelevant because Reeve—Mr. Perfect, Royce's older brother—asked her out! I wasn't even jealous.

Conveniently, we both went to the Cozy Theater to see "Jaws III"; me, on my first-ever date with Royce (or anyone, because I refused to count Craig) and Amy with Mr. Perfect. "Jaws III" was 3-D, but that was the only thing distinctive about it. It was all teeth. We had to wear weird cardboard glasses, and I hoped Royce wasn't looking at me when I had them on. The movie had no redeeming qualities.

Afterwards, we went to Amy's house to drink pop and eat popcorn. She served the best popcorn at her house with fluffy kernels and lots of real butter. When I was with Royce, Reeve didn't seem so intimidating. He was a comedian. I noticed how Royce had the same million-dollar smile as Reeve. Royce was taller and skinnier and gawkier than Reeve, who was every bit the smooth senior. Royce put his arm around me when we were sitting on the couch.

Jill came over, too. She was with three friends from Henning, a tiny town nearby known for a feed mill, a turkey hatchery, six Christian churches and its speed trap on Highway 210. All the friends were boys. I assumed she met them at a speech meet, but I wasn't sure. She acted bubbly, like she wasn't even thinking about Don. I was happy about that. After we joked around for a while watching Friday Night videos, she pulled me into Amy's windowless main floor bathroom and shut the door.

"That Dale guy said you were cute."

"Dale? On the bar stool?" I said.

"Yeah, with the blond hair. He said you were cute but Royce wasn't the kind of guy he expected to see you with."

"What does that mean?"

"I don't know. I thought you should know."

Our conversation reminded me of one I had with David Green earlier in the week when a bunch of us were horsing around before band practice. David had told everyone, "Royce Koroso was at the game and you know who was with him? Monica. And you know what he did? He had his arm around her." I didn't even know David saw us or would ever care to see who sat next to me. And why did he bother to mention it? It seemed like other guys were more attentive when I was attached. Only I didn't consider Royce and I attached. We were dating (sort of—was one date "dating"?). Definitely not "going together," and there was a difference.

I thought Dale's comment was weird. Royce was perfect for me. If we could ever get our kisses straight.

That night, I had a dream about Scott Briller. I dreamed he kissed the back of my neck, and then he stuck postage stamps to it. He licked the postage stamps like they were something beautiful, and pressed them to my skin, like I was a craft project. When I woke up, the hot feeling of being kissed stayed with me. I wondered why I dreamed about Scott, and I thought of how he cut my hair in ninth-grade science class. As I savored the dream, blinking my eyes to morning, that small act of violation felt sexy. But postage stamps? How kinky.

+ + +

"Believe it or not, I got in the house in ten minutes."

"I don't believe it," Jill deadpanned.

"No, really." I ignored Jill's sarcasm as I ran my fingers down the curly telephone cord trying to move the kink to the end. "Did you notice he had his arm around me the whole second half?"

"Yes, I noticed."

"It was his idea. But I liked it. After we had popcorn at Amy's, I was supposed to be in the house by 11:30. Scott, Paul Tanqueray and a bunch of other guys drove by when we were standing in my driveway so we talked to them for a while. Then I got two kisses and I went in the house. It was perfect."

"I don't get it, what's great about that?"

"Well, normally he stands around making stupid conversation and waiting for me to make a move."

"For longer than ten minutes?"

"Yeah, sometimes we stand in the driveway for more an hour."

"So Royce can't pull the trigger then?"

"Well, let's just say he's not like Brian Flourman."

"Isn't that a good thing? Wasn't Brian Flourman a little intense?"

"Yeah, I guess. In a good way. Do you think he'll come back?"

"Honestly? I didn't think you'd ever see him again after Labor Day weekend. And then he shows up out of the blue. If he came looking for you once, I bet he'll come again."

"Maybe he wants to ask me out."

"What about Royce?"

"Well, I'm not *going with* Royce yet."

After years of dying to have a boyfriend, I hesitated: I wanted to keep my options open. Reflecting on this dichotomy years later, I think I was as much in love with the *attention of* a boy at that point in my life as I was ever in love with a boy. Was that simply immature? Or was it irredeemably selfish?

I volunteered to lead the showcase committee for Spirit Week, scheduled to fall the same week as Valentine's Day every year. I cornered all the student council members and asked them to help clean out the showcases on Saturday morning. A half dozen display cases in the hallway across from the principal's office featured different displays every week or two. Usually, the DECA class[79] or cheerleaders decorated them, but during Spirit Week, the display cases highlighted the candidates for Spirit Week: kings and queens among the seniors, princes and princesses for the juniors, dukes and duchesses for us tenth graders and now, with the ninth graders in the high

---

[79] DECA stands for Delta Epsilon Chi and Distributive Education Clubs of America, but no one *ever* refers to the full name. At Wadena Senior High School in the '80s, DECA was a business and marketing class in which students liked to create informational 3-D displays. In retrospect, it probably would have been great training for my career path (which veered distinctly into marketing for a number of years) but when I was in high school I was paying more attention to boys than to business.

school building, we needed space for the counts and countesses. The featured royalty candidates filled the cases with pictures, trinkets, basketballs or pompoms and various other fluffy or sparkly tchotchkes that symbolized their high school experiences and personalities.

I worried I'd be the only one balling up construction paper and moving around glass shelves, but a crowd turned out to clean sweep. Even Todd-the-God, who didn't get home from the basketball game until midnight, showed up on time in all his feathered-hair glory. I asked him about the game, and he responded like a real person. He wasn't egotistical or snotty, just conversational. He was human after all, but even as we talked, I knew he wasn't flirting; he was simply being friendly, like he was with everyone. His breath-taking charm had eroded in the past year and a half, and I was no longer interested in chasing unattainable men. I was proud of myself for not being intimidated, for not clamming up like an idiot.

When I got home, all jazzed about completing my volunteer duties, the phone rang.

"Hi, is Monica there?"

I recognized Craig's voice immediately.

"This is she," I said slowly.

I didn't hang up, which was my first impulse, because I wanted to know why he was calling me.

"I'm only calling to tell you something." There was a long pause I didn't hurry to fill. "I'm sorry."

I couldn't believe it. In all the months since Craig had invaded my bedroom and tried to start conversations with me and then had gotten in trouble for peeping in Tonya Palomino's windows, Craig had never tried to apologize. In the pause after he said "sorry," I could hear him holding his breath. It was hard to hate him when I felt sorry for him.

"You're really a jerk, you know."

"Yeah, you're right."

I ended up accepting his apology and talking to him for an hour. I realized I had missed him and his goofy stories about playing Dungeons and Dragons with Mick and arguing with him about the relative superiority of Hall and Oates.

"Can we be friends again?" Craig asked, and I agreed. We had straightened out the mess Craig created when he invaded my space. I wasn't 100 percent sure I could trust him, but I was willing to give him a chance. It felt good.

+ + +

Brian Flourman showed up on my doorstep on a Wednesday evening. I had just gotten home from church choir practice and I was dancing around the living room to Michael Jackson's "Beat It" when I heard a knock on the door. There stood Brian Flourman, and his new-used Trans Am was parked in the driveway.

"Hey," he said coolly.

"Wow! It's you," I said, shocked and wondering how bad my hair looked. I felt like Cinderella must have when Prince Charming showed up out of nowhere holding her missing glass slipper. Only I didn't have Cinderella's presence of mind to invite him in.

"So," he said like a typical Minnesotan who started every sentence with "so." "So, I thought maybe you could show me around this hick town."[80]

He smiled a winning smile and his lips made me melt. I was dating Royce who I knew very distinctly was interested in me, but we

---

[80] Ah, so he got my letter and remembered how I had described my home town.

weren't going steady. Nothing was official, at least in my mind. For once, my *unencumbered* status was a positive thing.

"Sure, let me grab a jacket," I said, leaving the door open and running to the back of the house to grab a coat and avoid Mom and Dad's attention.

We hopped into the Trans Am, and I made all the proper comments about his car, which was an impressive upgrade from the rusty brown number he had been driving months ago. We drove all over Wadena, and I showed him Amy's house, the junior high, the high school, the Pizza Dena, the Cozy Theater, Dad's TV store and Hardee's. Eventually, I directed him to Sunnybrook Park, where I knew it would be deserted on a weeknight. Brian picked up on my signals, and he parked in a gravelly spot overlooking Whiskey Creek.

"Would you like some of my pop?" he said, handing me his 7up.

I accepted, and after having a gulp, I moved the paper cup to the drink holder of my car door instead of to the center console. Where it would have been in the way of what I was hoping was Brian's next overture.

"Want to practice kissing?" he said, like an attentive teacher.

"Sure, but I can't even sit next to you." The center console between the bucket seats of his Trans Am was nothing like the uninterrupted front seat of his other car. Ever the tender instructor, though, Brian moved back his driver's seat and showed me how to flip around to face him with my butt on the console and my legs draped over the passenger seat. This guy knew all the tricks.

We made out in his car for a half an hour. He wanted to give me a hickey, but I demurred.

Did I feel guilty? No. Did I like it? Absolutely. Was I embarrassed? For reasons I couldn't express then, yes, I felt shame. My attraction to Brian was entirely physical. In ways I hadn't yet articulated because I was so sexually inexperienced, I believed in my heart that physical intimacy should come with emotional intimacy. I liked Brian, sure, the same way I liked the eleventh grader—who was by now a senior—with the beautiful pink lips and silky hair. But I didn't *like* Brian the way I liked Royce, who was interested in *me*.

Brian drove me home and came into the house with me. The looks on my parents' faces betrayed their surprise, but they acted friendly and invited him to dinner sometime. My parents' affection for Brian's parents obviously extended to him.

I walked him back to his car and kissed him good night, one last quick French kiss imbued with desire but not meaning.

"I'll be back," he said.

When I confessed my escapade with Brian to Jill the next day, she was as aghast as she was when I told about French kissing with Brian the first time.

"What are you doing?!" she asked. "You supposedly want to go steady with Royce. Do you even know what 'going steady' means? It means you're going steady. *Steady*. It's not like you can turn 'steady' off and on like a faucet."

"Well, we're not steady yet. And Royce doesn't know about Brian."

"So? It's wrong. You can't go out and do things like that and be going steady with someone."

I had no response. Jill made me think. I liked Brian as a person, but I didn't like Brian as a boyfriend. I liked making out with him. I liked Royce like a boyfriend. And I liked making out with him. And I liked other guys, too. Doubts were fighting with conviction when it came to my loyalty to Royce.

Sunday, Sept. 4, 1983

Dear Diary,

They say a diary is a place to keep your feelings. Right now, I feel happy. All weekend I have been thinking about Royce. I think I truly like him. Royce is nice (and tall!) and easy to talk to. I get a funny feeling every time I think about him. This isn't like my romance with Scott. I hope it isn't. I don't want it to be. I guess we'll see how it goes.

24

I OPENED MY locker and lo and behold, inside sat a tiny pink teddy bear holding a heart-shaped note: "I love you."

It was from Royce.

"Love." Royce loved me. This was serious. Someday, such expressions of love would be as serious as marriage and mortgages. But right now, as I stood in front of my locker piled high with text books and the now-thick, yarn-tethered *A Novel Idea* and loose sheets of notes on American history and biological functions and half-written poetry, this creature in pink fur toted a message that made my heart flutter and my brain race.

Royce loved me!

Oh joy!

Royce loved me!

Oh no!

Wasn't this what I wanted forever and a day? A boyfriend? A boyfriend who liked me? Me and only me? And Royce was a good kisser, too.

He didn't have Brian Flourman's raw sexiness or his brother Reeve's smooth confidence or Scott Briller's dangerous air of mystery, but he liked me. He *loved* me! When Royce had his arms around me in the school hallway later in the day, he told me he wanted to go steady.

"Oh, you're sweet," I said, feeling conspicuous, as if everyone shuffling around us was looking at me.

"What do you mean?"

"Well, I just don't want to go steady. I feel sort of smothered."

Royce's face crumpled and his hold on me loosened considerably. "You want to break up?"

"No, I still want to go out with you. Just not steady."

"You want to go out with other guys?"

He had me cornered. I didn't want to admit I wanted to keep my options open. "No, I just don't want to go steady right now."

Royce dropped his arms and stepped back. "I've got to think about this," he said, like he had some choice in letting me go.

Our flourishing social lives crowded out such childish activities as slumber parties, but I corralled Jill, Amy and Cindy for a party in my Harvey Wallbanger basement for old time's sake. We took turns working our mojo in front of the Polaroid camera and a blow dryer for a homemade *Cosmopolitan* photo shoot. The pictures tell the story.

**THE DEER ANTLERS ON THE WALL ADD
A CERTAIN *JE NE SAIS QUOI*[81]**

In her usual cheeky fashion, Jill posed holding a pair of Adidas tennis shoes and pointing off camera like she was in a Sears catalog. Who needed glamour when laughs were far easier to elicit?

I felt a certain comfort, spending time with friends who knew me and whom I trusted. We gossiped over potato chips and homemade brownies.

"I have a hilarious story," Cindy said. "Mr. Jefferson insulted Tonya today in biology."

"I can't wait to hear this," I said.

"We had to weigh ourselves to prove some theorem," Cindy said. It didn't surprise me that she didn't know what they were proving. "Tonya said she didn't want to, and Mr. Jefferson said, 'Just think what you'd weigh if you had a brain.'"

---

[81] That is, "an inexpressible something, literally French for "I do not know."

I appreciated Mr. Jefferson's Superman sense of humor. "Ha, ha, ha!" No wonder I weigh so much, I thought.

"And then he said, 'Every class has to have at least one dumb blonde. Are you applying for the job?'"

We giggled. Served Tonya right. She was enticing, that was certain, and the boys couldn't get enough of her, but what a dummy.

"Did you hear?" Jill said. "Valerie is telling everyone she is having a boy."

"I can't believe she's pregnant," I said.

"My parents would kill me," Cindy said.

"I'm not surprised," Amy said. "I'm never having children."

"Me neither," I said, thinking about how I had to rock Baby Haskel to sleep not long ago. *That* was $3 well earned.

"You two are nuts," said Jill, ever the pragmatist.

I ripped paper from a spiral-bound notebook and passed it around. "Let's do slam books."

"Oh, I *hate* slam books," Cindy said. "Really?"

"Really. I need this," I said.

I wrote my headings across the top of the page. I didn't care about make-up tips that night (though my hair, that was different—all opinions on my hair were welcome). I wanted the *Truth* with a capital T. My friends obliged, and we wrote furiously for twenty minutes on the subjects of "hair suggestions," "clothes (be specific)," "public appearance," "extracurricular 'friends,'" "personality (be honest)," "overall comments (miscellaneous)" and, as if that wasn't enough, "one word to describe me." I looked up when I was trying to think of the right words to tell Jill she needed to try a new eyeshadow approach, and Amy's eyes met mine; she was looking for the right words to say something, too.

More important than eyeshadow, I wrote a heartfelt message to Jill about Don:

> I know it's hard to understand why someone as nice as you can't get a date except with a lying boozer. But that's not the way it will stay. I *really, really* like you. You deserve one *heck* of a nifty husband. Keep your hopes up. You are my very best friend in the whole wide world. Need I say more?

When I got my slam book back, I read it like a fortune teller reading tea leaves.

Hair suggestions:

Cindy: Your hair looked neat that night at the winter seasons dance.

Jill: I didn't *love* it when you took the crown of your hair and put in barrettes leaving the rest down. I do *love* the way you have it when it's in French braids.

Amy: I love it all curled up. But understand about the mist.

Clothes (be specific):

Cindy: You have good taste. I especially like how you coordinate your eyeshadow to match your outfits. Your Hang Ten shirt is excellent! Electric blue shoes? Well, maybe not.

Jill: I like your Gloria Vanderbilt jeans but you wear them too often. I love your Hang Ten shirt but I'm not into your bright red skirt with the lace (the one you wore with the blue shoes).

Amy: There's nothing I hate or even dislike about your whole wardrobe. Especially the blue shoes.

Public appearance:

Cindy: You usually are OK but sometimes you talk a bit loud.

Jill: Proud, confident and good-natured.

Amy: You sometimes talk, yell or laugh a little loud but hey, ya gotta get rowdy sometimes. Just make sure it's not all the time.

Monica's extracurricular "friends":

Cindy: I think that Royce and Greg are great! And, sorry to say it, but I think that Brent Gorgonzola has an inflated head!

Jill: Royce is sweet and Greg seems nice, too! No complaints here! Only slight jealousy! You're lucky to have someone so sweet and caring!

Amy: I honestly like Royce (as a friend), ha, ha. I also like his friends. It gives me something to do on the weekends.

Monica's personality (be honest):

Cindy: You aren't as moody as you used to be, which is good! Sometimes I have a hard time understanding your views (in general, nothing specific).

Jill: You're a great friend but a terrible enemy! Everything is always the other person's fault. You're always right and the other person is always wrong! Remember, you're smart but not perfect. But I'm still glad I'm your friend.

Amy: I was kinda upset earlier (in the afternoon) but that's my problem. Sometimes it seems as though you're high and mighty because you hang out with the student council.

Overall comments (miscellaneous):

Cindy: You are overall friendly and more popular than you know.

Jill: You have the most gorgeous nails I've seen! You are a good person to tell a problem to because your oohs and aahs are comforting. But remember, other people's insecurities are *monumental* to them!

Amy: I don't think you do it purposely, but you often leave Royce out when other (possibly cuter) guys come around.

***One* word to describe Monica**

Cindy: Understanding.

Jill: Self-assured.

Amy: Enchanting.

+ + +

I called Royce the next morning and invited him to Amy's that night. She hosted an impromptu pizza party. I brought *A Novel Idea* with me and handed it to Amy.

"I don't have time for that anymore," Amy said flatly. She was on my nerves anyway. I was still peeved that she'd called me "high and mighty" in my slam book. *She* was the high and mighty one. She was obsessed with her grades and had changed her class schedule all around so she didn't have to take Mass Media and get a B. She could take the last half of Trigonometry for credit and drop it next semester to take Chemistry II. Whoopee! I looked at her like she was crazy, *A Novel Idea* burning in my hands like a hot potato. I felt betrayed and insulted.

"OK," I said, shaking my head and stuffing the manuscript into the sleeve of my jacket so there wouldn't be a chance of forgetting it at Amy's.

Royce and I stayed at Amy's for a while and then went to my house to eat apple pie. Kay went to bed at 11:30 and left Royce and me watching "Night Tracks." Mom and Dad had long ago retired to their bedroom. Royce sat there with his arm around me until 12:10. Then I turned around sitting sideways—the way Brian had showed me in his car—with my arms around Royce. We exchanged a few words and a couple of kisses.

"Should we try a French kiss?" I asked nervously. Royce paused a long time. I hoped I didn't sound stupid.

"I've never done that before."

"That's OK, I'm out of practice."

So I went in, tongue hot. The first time wasn't satisfying. But the second one was better and the third one better yet. I didn't know where we were going with this, and I was nervous again. I didn't want to regret anything with Royce the way I did with Brian.

"It's late. You should go," I said.

He donned his leather jacket and we stood on the front porch and exchanged a goodbye French kiss.

I stepped inside and leaned against the closed door.

"This is wonderful," I thought. "We're over the hump. Now everything's hunky dory. Boy, do I like Royce!"

+ + +

"Amy doesn't want to write *A Novel Idea* anymore," I told Jill over the phone.

"I know. She told me."

"What should we do?"

"Finish it," Jill said.

"Be done?" I asked, incredulous.

"Yeah, it's time."

After I hung up the phone, I flipped through the handwritten pages of *A Novel Idea*. The story of Gwendolyn Joy Hayes was epic, in my humble opinion. She had been through so much rejection—dumped on every holiday, getting kissed by boys she didn't like and so many other high school challenges. But she had grown up in the pages of *A Novel Idea*, too, and I felt like the story needed an ending before I put it away. But besides the words "the end," I didn't quite know how to wrap up Gwendolyn's story satisfactorily. I cleared a spot on a high shelf in my bedroom closet and carefully stacked the pages of our progressive story.

+ + +

The next day, Royce left a note in my locker. He drew a heart around my name:

> Monica,
>
> How's it going? I'm doing good. Since yesterday, I've been totally happy. I don't think I've been *this* happy in a *long* time. But so you know … you know. I like you so much, it's indescribable. See ya later.
>
> Love you always,
> Royce

Predictably, guess who came to visit me: Brian Flourman. By then I realized he wasn't my Prince Charming. In some Minnesota Nice fashion, I told him to get lost. And I was glad I did. Though it would take years for me to internalize the mantra that "boyfriends are great but they are not life," and that "love isn't easy." Giving Brian the kiss-off was the beginning of learning the truth, that making out was fun but it wasn't as important as the relationship. I was doomed to repeat many of the mistakes I made The Year I Learned to French Kiss. But with Royce, I had something valuable: Royce was honest and genuine. Safe, too. Some days I liked Royce so-so and some days I liked Royce so much.

The love thermometer burst at the top one afternoon after the locker love note. It would soon be spring, and winter's thaw was beginning. The sidewalks were clear, wide-open spaces, beckoning pairs to walk two abreast instead of picking through unshoveled paths single-file. The trees lining the boulevards were still spindly and gray, but the promise of lush, green leaves hanging over the streets was at hand.

Walking me home from a dance where Royce had led me onto the tiled dance floor for every slow song and the melodic music flowed over us like the wavy lines of a daydream, Royce stopped and turned to face me. I could smell the faint aroma of Royce's woodsy musk cologne mingling with his unique bouquet. He looked into my eyes, clasped my hand and dropped his class ring in my palm.

"Let's go steady," he said. "I want you to wear my ring."

"I love it," I said, turning it over in my hands, fingering the forged basketball net on the side. It was heavy, with a black onyx stone, more expensive than most rings worn around the halls of Wadena Senior High School. *As soon as I get a spacer, I'll wear it all the time. But I can't lose it!*

I looked up into Royce's eyes. "Yes," I said. "I'd love to be your girlfriend."

The air smelled like spring: full of promise and new beginnings.

Sunday, Sept. 2, 1984

Dear Diary,

Tonight I called Royce and talked to him for a little bit. It's been one year since I met Royce. Boy, it was one heck of a year—but it was nice—much better than other years, I'm sure. Royce is a wonderful guy—that's a fact—but a tiny bit possessive. I really learned a lot anyway. About love, relationships, sex, etc. I'm definitely the better for it. Can I give it up? I doubt it ... But what about Brent? He's a sweety, too. I'm going to give both of them a try. See how long it lasts.

EPILOGUE

LIKE *A Novel Idea*, I was unable to tie up the loose ends of my high school love life with a pretty bow.

Royce and I dated—or I should say "went steady"—more or less happily throughout my junior year with a few dramatic break-ups and reunions thrown in for good measure. When school started again in September and I was a senior, I felt compelled to scratch the itch to play the field. Royce had become possessive and needy. He moped around all the time, lamenting his poor grades in anything math related, his performance on the basketball court, on the golf course and with me. Ostensibly, I wasn't attentive enough. The truth is, I wasn't. I didn't want to constantly stroke Royce's ego because I wanted the attention of other guys.

While I was mired in self-pity, I pulled out my old diaries. When I found the personal narrative I wrote for Mr. O back in eighth grade tucked into one of the pages, it was like sifting through an archeological dig, discovering some girl I barely recognized.

I like Brent Gorgonzola, food, my cat, clothes, tennis shoes and Judy Blume books. Oh, and rock-and-roll music.

I hate George Gordon, hyper dogs like my friend Amy's wiener dog, sometimes (almost always) my parents, low-heeled dress shoes and books with small print.

In the three years since writing that narrative, I'd finally admitted to myself I never liked rock-and-roll. I was a fan of pop music. And who was I to hate George Gordon? He was a nobody. I felt sorry for him and his greasy hair if I felt anything.

Brent-the-Cheese? He was another story. I still found him and his pouty lips appealing, and he acted like he might still be interested in me though he always respected the symbolism of Royce's ring, which I wore everywhere. I wondered what would have happened if we had bothered to pursue something after the French kiss under the street light.

After hemming and hawing in my diary ("Royce is a possessive brat and I can't stand it"), the drama reached a peak at Halloween. I was invited to a Halloween party that began with a string of printed clues leading all over town and ended with a VCR showing of "Parasite" at a fellow student council member's house. Royce hadn't been invited, and on our way home, he and Greg egged Jill's station wagon. In a heated discussion in the middle of the street, Royce admitted he supposedly "killed" Brent's house with eggs.

"Can I tell Royce that I can't possibly go out with such a destructive, immature possessive jerk and give up all I've shared with him in the past year?" I lamented to Dear Diary. "Or do I forgive him even though he said he'd do it again in a minute (he's not even sorry!) and, in a sense, condone his actions? I don't know what to think."

Over a pan of homemade brownies a few days later, Amy called me a bitch and told me Royce wasn't going to stand me much longer (what did she know?). "I can't pinpoint anything—it's just the little things," she said, picking crumb-clad chocolate chips out of her dessert. "All the biting little comments you manage to interject."

On Nov. 17, 1984, according to Dear Diary, I couldn't find Royce at basketball practice and learned he'd quit. Mr. 6-foot-3 had quit basketball! I went directly to his house for an explanation, and all he could say was that he wanted *more* from me. He said "more time," but privately I worried he meant more of something else and that he didn't think making out meant anything to me; we'd never ventured past third base. "I wish you wouldn't spend so much time with your friends," he said. "I feel like a chauffeur service."

I beat him to the punchline. "Royce, there isn't an *us* anymore. It's *you*. And *me*. There isn't love where there used to be. It isn't like it was before."

The last thing he said was "I frickin'[82] love you! But you don't care. Go ahead. Just leave."

My heart stopped when he said love.

"Goodbye, Royce." And I turned around and left.

As with previous breakups, I immediately second-guessed myself. "He didn't trust me. He is immature. He's not the guy I want to marry," I wrote in my diary. "So I did the right thing. Right?"

And poof! I was boyfriendless once again, and it lasted my entire senior year. Scott Briller, who had decided I wasn't girlfriend material

---

[82] You know what I mean when I wrote "frickin.'"

as soon as I had tried to fit into his partier scene[83], was a nonstarter. And as we had for four years, Brent and I played cat and mouse throughout my last year of high school but never consummated anything.

But that wasn't the worst of it.

Royce went straight from my arms into the arms of another. The very same "best friend" who had warned in her slam book messages to me that she found Royce "sweet" and that I "often leave Royce out when other (possibly cuter) guys come around" comforted Royce in his break-up sorrow with her friendship and, inevitably, her kisses (I taught him everything he knew!). Royce and Amy were an item within a week, and his class ring I had longed for and worn for months was on *her* finger.

Betrayed by Brutus[84].

Seeing Royce with anyone else would have bothered me, but no salt in the wound stung more than seeing Amy strut around with Royce on her arm. "I really hate Amy," I told Dear Diary (and anyone else who would listen). "I don't want to. But if I had the choice between being Amy's friend and living the rest of my life in Siberia, I'd learn Russian." Hating her surpassed even my desire to secure a new boyfriend, and I spent senior year imagining epic ways to tell her off (I bought a personals ad in the student newspaper that read, "Some friend you turned out to be. You know who you are." But I didn't have the courage to sign it). Mostly, I just stewed quietly in stagnant angry juices of my own creation.

---

[83] I learned this lesson at least and didn't drink another sip of alcohol for the remainder of high school.

[84] Marcus Junius Brutus stabbed Julius Caesar in the back on March 14, 44 BC. Caesar had declared himself *dictator perpetuo* ("dictator in perpetuity"), ticking off his Senate. Beware the Ides of March. And certain best friends.

Looking back, the truth I see is that I spent my emotional currency foolishly. I didn't genuinely want Royce from the very moment I had him as evidenced by initially brushing off his request to go steady. Amy only inherited my problems (she had no greater luck in improving his algebra grades than I had trying to help him with geometry). And my vitriol broke up the Hamster Cage forcing Jill and Cindy into the uncomfortable position of having to take sides. I guess funneling sorrow over my single status into hatred for Amy helped me get over Royce.

I had dared to love (and kiss) and had lost. I had been burned, and I didn't accept the double dare of *real* emotional engagement until I was in college. It was difficult for me to keep promises to romantic partners after Royce, and not keeping promises doomed me to a string of ultimately unsuccessful liaisons[85].

What intrigues me most about my diary accounts of 1982 is how little I learned and how often I have unconsciously repeated my mistakes in love and life. Ultimately, my experience French kissing Brian may have led, in some strange way, to my first marriage. Let me explain. With the limited experience I've collected over my years of being an adult, I have concluded one's first sexual experience echoes in all future encounters. I had a lover once who was obsessed with my hair; I found out his first lover had long hair that brushed his face while they were *in flagrante delicto*. So I believe the seeds of all fetishes are planted in people's first sexual experiences. However, I supposed *I* had no fetishes—that my first sexual experience was so innocent and vanilla, it had no echoes. Then I wrote this manuscript. I remembered, of course, learning to French kiss with Brian. As I read my diary I remembered we kissed in the room where he kept

---

[85] But that's another story. Or book.

his drums. I wrote this all down, still oblivious to my own biases. Then, as I was re-reading that chapter in the midst of revising what would ultimately become this book, it hit me: I *married* a *drummer*. The guy who introduced me to French kissing was a drummer, and I later fell in love with a drummer. That first marriage ended in divorce and as I penned my first memoir, *The Percussionist's Wife*, I tried to understand why I was so attracted to a man who was never committed to me and why I had been so blind to his flaws. Duh! Drummers were a fetish for me. Mystery solved.

Truth. Dare. Double dare. Promise. Or repeat. When I played that mostly innocent game for teenagers at Valerie's party in eighth grade, it became one of those before-and-after moments that defined my life like before college and after college or before saying "I do" and after saying "I do." Before the dare, my lips were chaste. After the dare, I learned kissing was so many things: Gross. Scary. Pleasurable. A part of an opposite-sex relationship but not representative of one. *Like* plus *kiss* didn't always equal love and, in fact, sometimes meant trouble.

Many years later when I was attempting to make room in the tiny closet I shared with my first husband in the tiny apartment we could afford after getting married, I decided to throw away those beloved blue satin ballet shoes, one of which I had been so bewildered to find when I rooted through my locker in ninth grade because Craig stashed it there. Brian had complimented them the night he taught me to French kiss. I had stood on my tippy-toes in them when Royce and I finally managed to kiss for the first time. Those uncommon shoes had given me style and confidence throughout high school and college and my first job as a newspaper reporter. By the time I uncovered them again in that tiny closet buried beneath a decade of newer footwear, they were literally falling apart. The toes were scuffed, the heels were frayed and the tough-as-nails plastic soles had holes in them. It was time to retire them. I gathered them up with all the other clothes and shoes that had outgrown their usefulness in my overfilled closet and unceremoniously deposited them in a dumpster in the apartment parking lot.

As I walked back into my tiny apartment, I reflected only briefly on what my once beautiful blue satin shoes represented. They landed me more than one prince[86] so they served me well. But I didn't need them anymore.

---

[86] And a few frogs.

Tuesday, Oct. 16, 1984

Dear Diary,

I got a Writer's Technique out of the library today. You know, I'd like to be a writer. I like culture. I like making "statements," and I like writing. Hmm... It would certainly be a challenge.

ACKNOWLEDGMENTS

THIS BOOK WOULDN'T exist except for the God-given discipline required to write in a diary nearly every day and the creativity in me that drives me to conjure something out of nothing. So thanks be to Judy Blume and to God!

My parents, however, do not have God's unlimited patience so they deserve thanks for being my rock, always dependable and loyal if sometimes unmoving. If my childhood horror stories are unremarkable, it's because they loved and protected me through all sorts of toddler and teenage tantrums and angst.

Jill deserves my gratitude for so many acts great and small since seventh grade but relative to this book, thank you for reading a first draft and providing feedback. After that preview, she suggested I market this book to the *Diary of a Wimpy Kid* crowd, which with its handwritten text and drawings would be the fifth-grade set. As usual, I didn't follow her sensible advice, perhaps to my own detriment.

I also would like to acknowledge Amy, Cindy, "Valerie," Brent, "Craig," "Scott," "Mick" and all the other members of Wadena Senior High School's Class of 1985 (and also select members of the

Classes of 1983 and 1984). Your role as characters in my story helped me tell it. And to those of you who didn't find yourselves here, I nonetheless hold many of you in high esteem. Many classmates are meaningful to me but didn't make the cut because they weren't relevant to telling the story of learning to French kiss. If you suspect you might be "Tonya," you're not; she is a composite character who is a tribute to all the Mean Girls in my life who were never as mean in real life as good fiction demands.

I want to acknowledge Brian for teaching me an important life skill (and other life lessons). Without you, this story would not have existed to be written. And "Royce," thank you for the fond memories I have of my first boyfriend and the first boy who told me he loved me. Even though I wasn't always appreciative of it back then, I am now.

My sister Kay, too, gets kudos for playing a less-fleshed out character here than she is in real life, for reviewing portions of this manuscript in many phases and for endlessly listening to me talk about hurdles in inspiration, writing and life.

Much gratitude goes to my advanced reviewers who took the time to review this manuscript and offer helpful suggestions.

And finally, I thank Brit Washburn for being my editor extraordinaire. She helped me separate the wheat from the chaff and inspired many useful additions to the emotional core of the story. And thanks to Mary B. Johnston who expressed such unabashed enthusiasm about a memoir about learning to French kiss and for putting me in touch with Brit.

To my loyal readers, I am indebted to you for spending your precious time with my writing. You make it all worth it.

ABOUT THE AUTHOR

MONICA LEE is the author of *The Percussionist's Wife: A Memoir of Sex, Crime & Betrayal* and *How to Look Hot & Feel Amazing in your 40s: The 21-Day Age-defying Diet, Exercise & Everything Makeover Plan.* She is a personal historian, blogger and writer whose work has appeared in Ohio and Minnesota newspapers and three anthologies. Follow news about *Truth, Dare, Double Dare, Promise or Repeat* and her other works at http://mindfulmonica.wordpress.com or catch up with her everyday life on her blog at http://minnesotatransplant.wordpress.com. She travels the country in an RV with her second husband and a miniature schnauzer that might be described as "hyper."

FOLLOW MONICA LEE:

- Author blog: https://mindfulmonica.wordpress.com/
- Everyday blog: https://minnesotatransplant.wordpress.com/
- Facebook: https://www.facebook.com/MonicaLee-Writer/

- Twitter: https://twitter.com/MNTransplant
- Instagram: https://www.instagram.com/mindfulmonica/

IF YOU ENJOYED *Truth, Dare, Double Dare, Promise or Repeat*, please consider leaving a review on Amazon or Goodreads, even if it's only a line or two. It helps independent authors and would be much appreciated.

OTHER BOOKS BY Monica Lee:
- *The Percussionist's Wife: A Memoir of Sex, Crime & Betrayal*
- *How to Look Hot & Feel Amazing in Your 40s: The 21-Day Age-Defying Diet, Exercise & Everything Makeover Plan*

OTHER WORKS IN which Monica Lee's writing has appeared:
- *When Bad Things Happen to Good Women: Getting You (or Someone You Love) Through the Toughest Times*
- *More Than a Coincidence: True Stories of Divine Intervention*
- *8 Slices of Cake*

READING GUIDE FOR MOMS & DAUGHTERS

ONE OF THE PURPOSES of this book, besides being a blast from the past for the author, is to spark conversations about relationships and sexuality among teenagers and their parents.

These are not easy conversations for most teenagers and a lot of parents. When I was growing up, I eschewed such discussions with my mother (and never entertained the concept with my father—never!); most of what I learned came from my friends and from books and magazines. But when I became a stepmother to a 12-year-old boy, I somehow became his confidant (an unexpected gift for which I am forever grateful). I was determined to be a worthy recipient of his trust and confidences. I employed three rules:
1. Always use anatomically correct language (while pretending, if I had to, to be unembarrassed).
2. Tell the truth.
3. Incorporate messages of morality when appropriate but refrain from judgment unless someone was endangered (fortunately, this never happened).

These rules served me and my stepson well, and I want to help other parents experience such forthright, meaningful conversations with their children. Use the following questions to inspire you:

> MONICA'S FIRST KISS occurred as the result of a dare, and she didn't like it. What was your first kiss like?
>
> SOMETIMES BRENT WAS mean to Monica, and sometimes Brent was sweet. Was Brent confused about his feelings for Monica or was Monica confused?
>
> MONICA SPENT A lot of time trying to impress boys. Did she spend enough time paying attention to her friends? Was she a good friend?
>
> MONICA FOUND FRENCH kissing with Brian to be thrilling, but Jill initially found it horrifying. Is French kissing gross? Why or why not?
>
> "WHAT SHE DOESN'T know can't hurt her," Monica told Brian when he confessed to having a girlfriend after teaching Monica how to French kiss. What do you think about Brian's behavior? Monica's?
>
> MONICA WAS REPEATEDLY victimized by Craig who broke into her locker and bedroom more than once and stole her belongings. Did Monica react appropriately? Did Monica's father do the right thing? What do you think of Craig? Has anyone ever invaded your boundaries in a way that made you feel uncomfortable?
>
> SCOTT SEEMED TO like Monica for her smarts rather than in spite of them, but she tried to impress him by behaving in a way

that was not true to her real character. What do you think about behaving in a way that is not you to attract the opposite sex?

MONICA BELIEVED HAVING a boyfriend would solve all her problems. Did it? How important to happiness do you think finding the right guy is?

IN THE EPILOGUE, Monica floats the theory that one's first sexual experience has echoes in all later ones. What about your first kiss or first sexual experience might reverberate?

MONICA BEGINS AND ends this memoir with descriptions of her favorite blue shoes. What do you think her blue shoes were a metaphor for?

www.ingramcontent.com/pod-product-compliance
Lightning Source LLC
Chambersburg PA
CBHW051750040426
42446CB00007B/291